SO-ABM-542

PEARY TO THE POLE

HARPER & ROW, PUBLISHERS
NEW YORK, EVANSTON, AND LONDON

A BREAKTHROUGH
BOOK

PEARY TO THE POLE

by Walter Lord

Illustrated with 27 Photographs

LIBRARY OF CONGRESS CATALOG CARD NUMBER: 63-9091

To John M. Woolsey III

CONTENTS

ILLUSTRATIONS

FOREWORD

In 1906 a thoughtful historian named John Chisholm Lambert wrote that once the North Pole was discovered, "it will be necessary for would-be explorers to sit down, like Alexander the Great, and weep because there are no more worlds to conquer."

Today we know better. The moon, the planets, the stars—there seems no limit. Yet distance is not the measure of discovery. Perhaps the greatest explorer of all was the first man daring enough to paddle his primitive raft beyond the sight of the land he knew.

In this sense, the discovery of the North Pole was a truly momentous event. For centuries men had wondered about it. For decades they had tried to reach it. For twenty-two years Robert E. Peary himself had been dazzled by the idea. When he finally triumphed, his success was more than personal—it was a historical "breakthrough," over-brimming with that inspirational quality always present when man achieves some long-sought goal.

Walter Lord

Robert E. Peary stands on the deck of his ship the *Roosevelt*. For Peary the North Pole was the goal of nearly a quarter of a century of desire and effort. In his fierce determination to reach the top of the world, his resourcefulness knew no limits. These furs, for instance, he adapted from the Eskimos. They were warm at $50°$ below zero, yet weighed no more than the clothes which the average man wears driving to work in the wintertime.

I   "FORWARD, MARCH!"

"Forward, march!" The command came in a crisp, clear voice that could be heard even above the howling wind. One by one a little group of fur-clad figures moved out across a jumbled sea of ice, each guiding a heavily laden sledge drawn by seven yelping, frisking dogs.

The group fell into single file and headed north. Above them, the stars danced and twinkled in the queer half-light of an Arctic day. Beneath them, the snow crunched to the tread of their feet. All around them stretched an endless waste of snow and ice. It was bitterly cold—50° below—so cold that a bottle of medicinal brandy, which one of the men tried to keep warm against his chest, was soon frozen solid.

Yet the men trudged on, heads bowed against the biting wind that slashed their faces, kept them from speaking, and all but hid them from view as it whipped the powdered snow into a fine icy dust. Bringing up the rear was the man who had ordered them forward, ready to throw his support wherever needed.

His name was Robert Edwin Peary, and he was a commander in the United States Navy. He was a big man with bristling moustache and steel-gray eyes that peered through the fringe of his hooded jacket. Hampered by his furs, he moved slowly, but his heart beat fast, for on this first morning of March, 1909, he was setting out to achieve his life's dream: to be the first man ever to reach the North Pole.

Now it lay only 413 miles ahead. Not much as distances go—about as far as Boston to Washington—but these were miles of solid ice. Worse, it was not ordinary ice . . . the kind that covers a pond or stream. This was sea ice—the frozen surface of the Arctic Ocean itself. Strange tides and currents were always at work, leaving treacherous gaps of inky water that seemed just waiting to swallow somebody up. But Peary didn't hesitate as he pushed steadily on.

Behind lay the more familiar world he knew. First, there were the empty igloos at Cape Columbia, the jumping-off place his men had just left. Then, ninety miles behind these, there was the base ship *Roosevelt*, moored at Cape Sheridan, the farthest north a boat had ever gone. And still farther behind were other things: The memories of twenty-two years of Arctic work, seven expeditions, six attempts on the Pole itself—each defeated by some unexpected, agonizing turn of events.

Could Peary do it this time? Common sense said no. He had always failed. Yet man can profit by failure too, and buried in these past defeats were lessons . . . important lessons that one day might lead to success.

II "THE THING THAT I MUST DO"

It was twenty-five years earlier when Robert E. Peary first thought of standing at the top of the world. And it happened not in the frozen north but in the sunny Caribbean.

He was sailing to Nicaragua in 1884 as a young United States naval engineer. At this time there was no canal between the Atlantic and Pacific, and Peary was on a trip to study where one might be built. But as his ship passed the little island of San Salvador his mind was far from canals.

This distant shore had been Columbus's landfall

4

on his first trip to the new world. Now the very sight filled restless twenty-eight-year-old Peary with excitement. What a thrill to have been Columbus! Here was a man, Peary wrote that night in his diary, "whose fame can be equalled only by him who shall one day stand with 360 degrees of longitude beneath his motionless feet and for whom East and West shall have vanished—the discoverer of the North Pole."

At the time it was only natural to think of the Pole this way. The vast, empty Arctic had intrigued men for centuries. At first people hoped that this maze of frozen seas and islands might hide a short cut from Europe to the riches of the Far East, and a long line of explorers searched in vain for what they called "the Northwest Passage." Gaspar Corte-Real was doing this for the Portuguese as early as 1500; Henry Hudson was at it for the English in 1610; each country had its heroes.

Later men knew they would never get to the Orient that way, but the fascination of the Arctic remained. It was so big, so dangerous, so unknown. The very mystery of it beckoned anyone who yearned for fame and adventure. But the price was often high. In 1845 Sir John Franklin led two small ships into the ice far north of Hudson's Bay—they were crushed by the floes and all 129 men were lost. In 1879 Lieutenant De Long of the American Navy took another small ship, the *Jeannette*, through the Bering Straits and into the ice far north of Siberia. It too was crushed, and nearly all were lost. In 1881 a young United States Army officer named Adolphus Washington Greely led a small expedition to Fort Conger, to the west of northern Greenland; three years later only six of forty-two survived.

So it went. But each failure only stirred others to greater effort. Gradually most of the Arctic was explored, mapped, and charted, until at last only one final mystery remained—the greatest of all—the North Pole itself.

This now became the goal of everyone. Rich men like Lord Northcliffe of England poured in money. Royalty like the Prince of Monaco and Italy's Duke of Abruzzi gave their support. Danes, Russians, Americans, explorers from many nations joined the race to get there first. Every conceivable theory was tried—new bases, new kinds of ships, food, and clothing—but in the end the ice and cold always proved too much. Dozens tried, but the Pole remained just out of reach . . . ever more tantalizing, ever more challenging and mysterious.

What was it like anyhow? Knowing nothing, men could only imagine. In early times some people felt the Garden of Eden lay at the Pole—a lovely sunlit land magically protected by the barriers of ice and snow. Others claimed they might find there the fabled lost continent of Atlantis. Many assumed that the Pole was not only on land but full of fabulous riches—great untouched deposits of gold and other precious metals. The Eskimos, listening to the explorers talk about the globe spinning on its axis, thought that the Pole was marked by a real spike sticking out of the earth. They even called the Pole "the Big Nail."

It was all so exciting to dream about, and Robert E. Peary was just the man to fall under the spell. From his earliest days he was immensely romantic. Born in Pennsylvania in 1856, he was soon taken by his widowed mother to Maine, where he grew up, a sensitive boy who loved to write about songbirds and the beauty of the sunrise. He liked poetry too and wrote long, romantic verses about knights and fair ladies. Later he composed valentines, full of flowing grace, and once designed a Christmas card showing a pretty girl floating through the sky on a snowflake. It was only natural that such a boy should also feel the romance of the mysterious, undiscovered North Pole.

Other men, of course, dreamed about the Pole too, but most were only dreamers. What made Peary different was his immense determination. As a boy he drove himself tirelessly on long mountain hikes. At Bowdoin College he fought hard to win a place on his class crew. In his studies he worked equally hard, sometimes staying up all night just to finish some classroom problem. He proved a brilliant engineering student, once graded a railroad perfectly without any previous experience.

He was just as industrious and practical after graduation, when he joined the Navy as a young engineer. He quickly impressed his superiors with bright new ideas for building a pier and designing canal locks. He was, in short, not only the kind of man who might dream about the North Pole but might eventually do something about it.

But not yet. Right now, as his ship steamed by San Salvador and headed on for Nicaragua, Peary had his present job to do. So he put aside his dreams of polar conquest and turned to the problem of surveying a transoceanic canal.

All that winter and spring he worked at it. Again and again he showed that streak of stern determination. To make the best survey possible, he struggled through swamps and jungles where no white man had ever been before. During the hot, sticky days he often worked in muddy water up to his waist. In the dripping nights he slept on the ground under a rubber blanket. At last the job was done, largely due to his skill and energy.

Back in Washington in the summer of 1885, Peary felt for his first time the sting of disappointment. No money could be found to go ahead with the canal, and the entire project collapsed. All that work for nothing! Brooding over it, Peary walked along a street one night, aimlessly dropped into a bookstore and began to browse. His fingers idly leafed through the pages of a little pamphlet on the great inland ice of Greenland—a vast glacial sea that no one had ever explored.

Suddenly all the excitement of the Arctic came surging back. Once again he dreamed of the Pole and the unknown region around it. What secrets lay locked in those vast Greenland ice fields? What mysterious force steadily pushed the ice to the coast, where it broke off in huge chunks that drifted south as icebergs? Did the ice reach all the way across Greenland? Did it stretch clear to the Pole? Could a man use it as a great highway to reach the top of the world?

He must see. He had no experience—little matter, that hadn't helped other explorers. He had no reputation—he boldly approached the National Academy of Science anyhow and by the sheer force of his personality won the Academy's interest. He had no free time—somehow he wangled six months' leave from the Navy. He had no money—he borrowed $500 from his mother.

In May, 1886, he was on his way. Taking a steam whaler, he landed on Disko Island, near the west coast of Greenland. Here he found a young Danish official named Christian Maigaard. Peary quickly persuaded the Dane to join him. The two men soon crossed to Greenland and headed inland onto the ice cap. With luck perhaps they could go all the way to the east coast. But it was slow going over the ice, and finally their food ran out. Reluctantly Peary turned back.

There was no denying it was a defeat. They had gone only a hundred miles, not nearly far enough to learn whether the ice cap stretched to the Pole. But there were consolations. Peary now knew that two of his pet theories about expeditions were sound—keep them small and travel light. And he knew something else too: he was more convinced than ever that this was his life's work. He may have been defeated this time, but he would be back.

In Washington again, Peary immediately began planning his next expedition. But then came two interruptions. First, the canal project was revived, and in 1888 Peary made another survey trip to Nicaragua. Then came an even bigger complication. He fell in love.

She was a pretty Washington girl named Josephine Diebitsch, and Peary married her on a blazing August day in 1888. The event naturally raised the question, what would marriage do to his plans for the Arctic? Might he not give it all up, settling for a blissful life at home with his bride?

Instead he took her along. On June 6, 1891, Peary again set out for Greenland, this time with his wife and five hand-picked assistants. By now the Danish explorer Fridtjof Nansen had already succeeded in crossing the Greenland ice cap, so Peary could no longer have the honor of being first. Little matter, he would cross farther north. This would be much more useful in exploring the best route to his ultimate goal, the North Pole.

Misfortune struck almost at once. On July 11 the expedition's little ship *Kite* was steaming through the frozen seas off Greenland when an icecake crashed against the rudder. The heavy iron tiller swung wildly over . . . smashed against Peary's leg, snapping the bone just above the ankle.

The crew carried him below, where the expedition's surgeon quickly set the break. It was a good job, for the doctor was very skillful. He was a pleasant, hard-working young man from Brooklyn, New York. His name—Frederick A. Cook.

Thanks to Dr. Cook's fine care, Peary was soon comfortable. But it was a serious blow. It was difficult enough to explore the Arctic with two sound legs; it was almost impossible with one of them broken. Should he turn back?

Peary never hesitated. He grimly ordered the expedition forward, as if nothing had happened. When the ship reached Greenland, he had himself taken ashore, strapped to a plank. Lying there, he directed his men as they unloaded the ship and built the camp. After five weeks he was limping about. His determination carried him along again.

All that following winter of 1891–92 Peary prepared for his trip across Greenland. He led his men on hunting trips, taught them to build sledges and handle dog teams. The men found him blunt and tactless much of the time but always gentle when they were in trouble. There was the time, for instance, when he and Dr. Cook were caught in a blizzard while probing the ice cap. As Cook began to freeze, Peary dug a hole in the snow, put the doctor in it, and covered the makeshift shelter with his own trousers. Then to give still greater protection, Peary wound himself around the windward side of the hole till Cook revived.

On May 3, 1892, Peary finally started out. The

supporting party soon turned back, and Peary continued on with only one companion. Day after day they pushed across the ice cap. Sometimes the blinding glare made it impossible to see; other times the driving snow and bitter winds made them long for the glare again. But on July 4 they finally stood on the northeast coast. They had come five hundred miles, completely across Greenland.

What did it prove? From the lay of the coast Peary now knew that Greenland was an island, that the ice cap itself was no path to the North Pole. But he still didn't know what role this vast empty area might play in helping him reach the target. Just to the north lay more land. Actually this was an extension of the Greenland coast, but to Peary it looked like a new set of islands. Might they be used as stepping stones to the Pole? There was no more time to explore this year, but he must come back.

Next spring, 1893, he again wangled leave from the Navy, and headed north early in June. This year he took eleven men. Dr. Cook didn't come, but an equally valuable member of the last expedition was on hand again. This was Matthew

Henson, a Negro helper who had been with Peary since the days in Nicaragua. By now he was a fixture on these trips.

Mrs. Peary came again too, and the expedition gained still another member when she had a little daughter at the base camp in Greenland. This was the farthest north a white child had ever been born, and the world took great interest in her. Christened Marie Ahnighito Peary, she was promptly nicknamed "the snow baby."

March, 1894, and Peary started across the Greenland ice cap again. Once more he headed for the northeast coast, still hoping the land to the north might be an island group that would help him reach the Pole itself. But he never found out. He had set out too early, and a raging winter blizzard soon killed many of his dogs and crippled his men. They were lucky to get back to camp alive. A bitter defeat, but he had two years' leave and resolved to try again next spring.

April, 1895, and he set out with Matthew Henson and a young man named Hugh Lee. This time they started late enough, but in the Arctic disaster can strike in many ways. First, they couldn't find the food they had stored along the

Marie Ahnighito Peary was born farther north than any other white child in history. In the fall of 1900 she and her mother came to the Arctic to spend the winter with her father during the 1898–1902 expedition. "The snow baby" was then seven years old, and it was her fourth season in the North. This picture was taken the next spring.

16

early part of the route—it was hopelessly buried in the snow. Then the hunting turned bad. Again and again, they seemed to face retreat or starvation. Again and again, they went on anyhow. Again and again, they found a musk ox or an Arctic hare just in time. Raw meat, torn from the warm body of a freshly killed musk ox, came to seem like a treat.

At last they reached the northeast coast, but so weak they could do no more. There was absolutely no hope of the Pole. Defeated again, Peary led his men back across the ice cap. They could find no food and even had to eat some of their dogs. Lee grew desperately sick, finally lay down to die, begging the others to go on without him. "We'll have no more of that kind of talk," Peary scolded him, "we will all get home or none of us will."

They finally stumbled into their west coast base camp two weeks later. The three men were starving, and only one dog was still alive. Peary took him in his arms and began feeding him great chunks of deer meat. Only when he was sure the dog was full, did he look for something to eat himself.

As the party headed wearily back for New York, there was only one bright spot. Peary had again shown his determination, his toughness, and his curious gentleness in adversity. Important qualities, but not enough to console the leader himself. He could only promise that he would return.

In 1896 he was back again, but this time his plans were less ambitious. He had no money for a full-scale expedition, so he merely picked up two meteorites found on his earlier trips. It was the same story in 1897, when he collected a third meteorite. But both years the Pole was never out of Peary's mind. By now it had become an obsession, crowding out everything else. It was "the goal of the world's desire . . . the one dream of my life."

And in 1898 he tried again. His past feats made it easier this time to get support. Fifteen private backers raised $60,000 and were soon organized into the Peary Arctic Club. More good news came when the English publisher Lord Northcliffe contributed a ship. But success has its drawbacks too. Peary now found it almost impossible to get leave from the Navy. His Arctic work was on his own time, and high-ranking officers—jealous of his growing fame—tried to keep him on duty.

Finally his friend Charles A. Moore, a powerful backer of President McKinley, went straight to the White House. "You remember, Mr. McKinley, you said to come to you if I ever wanted anything?"

"I do," sighed the President, expecting something costing millions.

"I want Lieutenant Peary of the Navy granted five years' leave to continue his great work in the North."

"Oh, is that all?" McKinley laughed. "Of course I'll do it."

So by fall of 1898 Peary was back in the Arctic, this time based at Cape D'Urville on Ellesmere Island. He had now given up his plan to assault the Pole from Greenland—this island to the west seemed easier and perhaps nearer. Plunging into his work, Peary soon showed he had lost none of his bluntness. Exploring the wilderness west of Kane Basin, he unexpectedly met the Norwegian explorer Otto Sverdrup. Peary had long felt Sverdrup was encroaching on his own project, and although the two parties were the only human beings within hundreds of miles, he refused to join Sverdrup in a cup of coffee. It was a slight the Norwegian was not to forget.

Peary was soon hard at work shifting supplies to his advance base at Fort Conger. This had been the headquarters of the ill-fated Greely expedition seventeen years before, and a small wooden shack offered some protection against the cold. It was 250 miles nearer the Pole than Peary's main base—but that also meant 250 miles of danger while bringing up the supplies.

Arriving with a fresh load one bitter night in January, 1899, Peary felt a wooden numbness in his toes. He knew all too well what it meant. They were frozen. . . .

Racked with pain, he soon was lying on a cot in the hut. Shivering in the darkness, he knew only that most of his toes would have to come off, that this could spell the end of his hopes. Raising himself on his elbow, he fiercely scrawled on the walls some Latin words he remembered from school: *"Inveniam viam aut faciam"*—"I shall find a way or make one."

They took him back to the ship, amputated eight of his toes, urged him to return to New

York. Instead he wedged strips of tin in the soles of his boots, stuffed them with straw to cushion the pressure, and soon was hobbling north again.

Spring, 1900, and he launched another assault on the Pole. But it had taken too long to shift his supplies, and once again he started too late in the season. Melting ice blocked him at every point, and he was forced to explore the north coast of Greenland instead.

Spring, 1901, and he was trying again. But the long Greenland trip had taken its toll. His men were still exhausted, and after a week of small progress, he called off the drive.

Spring, 1902, and he tried once more. This time everything seemed to go wrong. Six Eskimos with him died. Much of his food ran out. His advance base at Cape Sabine proved much too far from the Pole. Pushing on anyhow, he was stopped on the sea ice by dangerous lanes of open water. Defeated again, he gloomily wrote in his journal: "The game is off. My dream of sixteen years is ended . . . I have made the best fight I knew. I believe it has been a good one. But I cannot accomplish the impossible."

But of course he was coming back. He couldn't

stay away, whatever he might write in a moment of discouragement. He returned to New York but within two years was preparing a fresh attack on the Pole.

In July, 1905, Peary—now a commander— started north again. This time he had a couple of new advantages. First, Theodore Roosevelt was now in the White House. The buoyant young President loved courage, determination, and any exciting adventure. Peary was a man after his own heart. The Government still put up no money, but this time the Navy officially sponsored the expedition.

The commander also had a new ship, thanks to the ever-faithful Peary Arctic Club. She was named the *Roosevelt* after the enthusiastic President, and she was designed especially for his needs. Her powerful engines could drive her through the thickest ice. Her thirty-inch wooden sides, sheathed in steel, could ward off the heaviest chunks. Her sharp steel prow could cut through the floes, or rise high and slam down again, crunching the ice to bits. She was a ship that would not have to be based hundreds of miles from the Arctic Ocean but could batter her way through to Cape Sheridan, putting him less than five hundred miles from the Pole itself.

She did her part too, and with this great advantage Peary again attacked the Pole in the spring of 1906. Leaving the ship at the Cape, he continued north with his sledges. At first all went well, but then, far out on the sea ice, he was again blocked by those shifting lanes of open water that Arctic men call "leads." He finally got by and pushed on to $87° 6'$—the farthest north any man had ever reached.

But not far enough. He was still 174 miles from the Pole, and his men were exhausted, his food almost gone. Defeated again, he had to turn back. It was no consolation that he had come closer than any other man. To Peary, his new record was "but an empty bauble compared to the splendid jewel on which I had set my heart for years, and for which on this expedition I had almost literally been straining my heart out."

The trip back to the *Roosevelt* was harrowing; the voyage back to New York even more so. Despite her stout construction the ship was nearly crushed by the ice. She lost her rudder, then her stern post, then part of her stem. Her propeller

Captain Bob Bartlett (right) stands with Peary on the *Roosevelt*. Bartlett began his work with the explorer during the 1898 expedition. This is an unusual picture, for the captain is without his pipe. Normally it was almost a part of him. He was the only man Peary allowed to include tobacco in the carefully planned sledge loads.

was bent and twisted. Food and fuel ran low, and a great storm off Labrador nearly carried her mast away. It often looked hopeless, but Peary merely told his skipper Bob Bartlett, "We've got to get her back, Captain, we're going to come again next year."

But determination alone is not always enough, and this was one of those times. Back in New York misfortunes continued to pile up. His backers began to lose heart, and his money ran low. The battered *Roosevelt* needed an expensive overhaul. Then a new set of boilers failed to arrive on time, forcing Peary to postpone his plans for 1907. On top of everything came the death of Morris K. Jessup, head of the Peary Arctic Club, who was to pay for the boilers and much, much more.

Preoccupied with these disasters, Peary paid little attention to another sailing for Arctic waters in the summer of 1907. His old colleague Dr. Cook was heading north with a millionaire sponsor named John R. Bradley, ostensibly on a hunting trip. Even after Bradley returned and announced that Cook was really going for the Pole, Peary took only scornful note. The doctor had no ship, little equipment, and less organization.

Peary still felt there was only one man destined to conquer the Pole, and that was himself. If not this year, then certainly next year. Somehow he would find the money he needed, for as he told the members of the National Geographic Society at a dinner in his honor: "The Pole is the thing which it is intended that I should do, and that I must do."

III "I SHALL WIN THIS TIME"

Stirred by Peary's determination, a Mr. Turnbull of New Orleans offered the explorer a novel suggestion: take an automobile and drive to the Pole. The car would have detachable wheels. These could be replaced with either sled-runners or pontoons—whichever might be useful.

The whole nation wanted to help. People everywhere showered Peary with ideas. One man suggested that he lay a pipe line and have hot soup pumped to his men as they advanced on the Pole. Another urged him simply to skate there.

Another advised him to use a tractor which would jump the leads of open water by means of an attached balloon.

Another wanted Peary to build a sawmill at the base camp, then cut boards for a blizzard-proof tunnel—but he never said where Peary could find wood in the Arctic. Another came up with a mysterious cannon guaranteed to lob the explorer direct to the target—but he never said how Peary would get back. The commander was especially amused by one man who had the absurd idea of going to the Pole by submarine.

Actually no one was ever in less need of advice. Peary knew exactly what he wanted to do. His past attempts had not been wasted. Each one taught him some new lesson. By now he had a plan that he was sure would work.

First, he would push the *Roosevelt* as close to the Pole as possible. He would again smash through the ice to Cape Sheridan, some 350 miles farther north than Kane Basin, the base used by other explorers. This had worked last time and had nothing to do with his defeat.

Next, he would make the most of his friendship with the Eskimos. Through the years Peary had grown very close to a small tribe that lived on Smith Sound. He gave them knives, tools, and rifles. In return they supplied him with dogs; they helped him hunt; they taught him to drive their sledges, wear their furs, build their igloos. Now he would rely on these Eskimos as much as possible. After all, they lived in the Arctic and ought to know best—a simple idea that never occurred to other explorers.

Finally, he would use a carefully organized system of pioneer and supporting teams. Peary had been working on this for some time, and each past failure showed something which should, or should not, be done in the future. Now he felt he had it right. He would break up his party into several independent "divisions." One would go ahead, making the trail and building igloos. The rest would follow about a day behind. This main party would be broken into divisions too— Peary's and those supporting him. As the supporting divisions used up their supplies, the near-empty sledges would be sent back, always with the men and dogs in poorest condition. Finally only Peary's team would be left—less than 150 miles from the Pole—fresh and ready for the final dash.

Peary was sure his plan would work, but what he didn't know, and what no helpful letter told him, was where to find the money. It had cost $75,000 to refit the *Roosevelt*, and now the Peary Arctic Club's treasury was empty. There was nothing left to pay the crew or buy food and fuel for the long trip north. Desperately Peary begged, scraped, spent the last of his own funds— "all my personal means, all I could save, some $80,000."

As usual his determination finally won out. Just when things looked darkest, Mrs. Morris K. Jessup—widow of his strongest backer—sent in a generous check. Others, won by the sheer doggedness of the man, sent more. His money problems were solved.

A final hurdle remained. Jealous officials in the Navy Department once again tried to block Peary's leave. But this time his friend Theodore Roosevelt rushed to the rescue. A stern word from the White House and all Navy resistance vanished. Writing his thanks, Peary assured Roosevelt, "I believe that I shall win this time, and I believe that this is the work for which God Almighty intended me."

His way cleared at last, Peary now turned to recruiting his men. Again past experience was paying off—he knew just what he wanted. Small, wiry men were best; heavyweights ate too much, took up too much room, were more likely to break through thin ice. As for character, his team should be self-reliant and above all cheerful. The Arctic was no place for a gloomy misfit.

"If you are still interested in Arctic exploration," ran the telegram to Donald B. MacMillan, a young prep-school master at Worcester Academy, "come to see me at once, Grand Union Hotel, New York City." Peary had known about MacMillan for years, and he was just the type needed—the deserving son of a ship captain lost at sea, a star athlete at the commander's own alma mater Bowdoin. His character and physical ability were both well known.

Matthew Henson, Peary's Negro servant, was another natural. He had been along on all but one of the commander's polar trips. By now he was an excellent sledge maker and a superb dog driver.

Captain Bob Bartlett had taken the *Roosevelt*

Ross Marvin, a thirty-four-year-old Cornell engineering graduate, was Peary's expert on mathematics and meteorological work. Liked and respected by everyone, he was heading for a mysterious end not at all in keeping with his calm, open manner.

Matthew Henson was already an experienced seaman when he first met Peary. An invaluable assistant, he built sledges for the 1908 expedition, converted stoves from kerosene to alcohol, showed new men how to handle dog teams, and acted as interpreter for the party. Fond of the Eskimos, he adopted the orphaned Kudlooktoo in 1893.

up and back on the 1905–06 expedition. He was only thirty-three but of old Newfoundland stock —the Arctic practically ran in his blood.

Ross Marvin, Peary's secretary, had also been along last time. He was a brilliant young Cornell engineer, an expert on weather and tides.

Dr. J. W. Goodsell was new, but he had the kind of pioneer background Peary liked. Also, he specialized in microscope work. That ought to be useful in medical research.

But there was nothing logical about Peary's selection of the sixth and last man for his team. Twenty-two-year-old George Borup was chosen purely on whim. One year out of Yale, Borup had a clean, carefree charm that made him still seem a boy. He had tried working for the Pennsylvania Railroad but hated the routine. He loved sports and outdoors, and soon began hounding Peary to go along on the trip. For a while it was a futile but imaginative campaign. Once he even sent the commander a telegram that said, "Have just shot a hole-in-one—now will you take me?"

Peary finally granted an interview, and Borup appeared at the Grand Union Hotel, uncomfortably neat in a new gray suit. The outcome was

Donald MacMillan was a young schoolmaster making his first trip to the Arctic, but the far north had always fascinated him. He missed going on Peary's 1905 trip only because he had promised to teach the next school year. In 1908 he was free to leave, and this time there was no holding him back. During the grimmer moments of the expedition, Matt Henson described him as being "the life of the funeral."

Photograph by Robert E. Peary © Robert E. Peary, Jr., and Marie Peary Stafford, courtesy National Geographic Society

George Borup was another newcomer to Arctic work. One year out of Yale and bored with a routine railroad job, he won a place on the expedition through a combination of persistence and the pleading of his father. Borup's enthusiasm more than made up for his inexperience.

Courtesy of The Explorers Club, New York City

inevitable. The expedition was already full . . . Borup had no experience whatsoever . . . he contributed nothing but desire—so Peary told him to come along.

The dull world of the railroad business soon lay far behind as Borup sweated on a Manhattan pier in the hot June sun, loading supplies on the *Roosevelt*. The variety was enough to stir anyone's love of adventure—snow knives, hammocks, pickaxes, rifles, moccasins, candles, dog traces, dynamite for blasting the ice.

The windlasses clanked on: 800 pounds of tea; 100 cases of condensed milk; 16,000 pounds of flour for ship's biscuits; 30,000 pounds of pemmican. All were absolutely essential, but Peary gave special attention to the pemmican. He believed that this concentrate of beef, fat, and dried fruit was the most nourishing food for Arctic work. He had it packed in different colored containers —blue for men, red for dogs. For easier carrying he ordered the length of the package to be exactly the same as the width of a sledge. And even after the contents were eaten, the containers were designed to be used as building blocks. It was another example of the commander's thoroughness.

Now sailing day was almost at hand, and even Captain Bob Bartlett began to sense the excitement. These trips were an old story to him—yet always new. Who dared guess what fresh peril or surprise lay ahead? Puffing on his inevitable pipe, he watched the men load the ship and felt once again "the suspense and eagerness that go before an Arctic expedition."

It was a feeling shared by the whole country. In the twenty-two years since Peary began trying, the world's interest in the Pole had reached fever pitch. Everyone rejoiced when Norway's Fridtjof Nansen almost succeeded in drifting across the Pole in his little ship the *Fram*. All shuddered when the Swedish aeronaut Salomon August Andrée died trying to get there by balloon. As America's best-known entry in the polar sweepstakes, Peary had become a national hero—much like an astronaut fifty years later.

Now the nation showered the *Roosevelt* with gifts: books, magazines, games, even a billiard table. Peary, never at ease with people, inwardly seethed at the jumble of useless presents. But there was nothing he could do, except silently swear that he would throw the whole mess overboard

On July 7, 1908, the *Roosevelt* anchored at Oyster Bay, Long Island, where Commander and Mrs. Peary had lunch at the summer home of President Theodore Roosevelt and his family. Afterward, the President, his wife, and his sons, Theodore Jr., Kermit, and Quentin, came to inspect the ship. In this photograph, President Roosevelt (middle foreground) talks to a group of reporters and photographers on the foredeck of the ship. Peary can be seen farther back, to the right.

once out of sight of land. Meanwhile the crowds swarmed around the pier, cheering the men and the ship.

"I'll see you up there," called a waterfront loafer, as the crowd waved good-bye on the afternoon of July 6. Slowly the stubby, black *Roosevelt* pulled away from her pier and swung into the current of New York's East River. It was the hottest day of the year, but the blazing sun didn't wilt the enthusiasm that swept the harbor. Thousands cheered along the shore . . . every whistle seemed tied down . . . the presidential yacht *Mayflower* banged away with its signal gun. As the ship passed the city jail on Blackwell's Island even the prisoners swarmed to their windows and waved.

On to Oyster Bay, where next day President Roosevelt inspected the ship named in his honor. Swinging over the rail, Roosevelt gave no thought to dirtying his white duck suit. He was much too curious. No president has ever had wider interests or greater enthusiasm than Theodore Roosevelt, and this was a day after his own heart. He squeezed into Peary's tiny cabin. He tumbled down into the engine room. He patted the Es-

President Roosevelt looks down into the hold at the Eskimo dogs which Peary raised on Eagle Island, Maine. The President's youngest son, Quentin, is at the left. Bob Bartlett stands on Roosevelt's right.

kimo dogs. He shook hands with every member of the crew. The air rang with his favorite cry, "Bully!"

At last it was time to say good-bye. "Mr. President," Peary declared, "I shall put into this effort everything there is in me—physical, mental, and moral."

"I believe in you, Peary," Roosevelt replied, "and I believe in your success, if it is within the possibility of man." And then he was gone.

The breeze quickened, the rigging hummed as the *Roosevelt* picked up steam and turned north. Behind lay the speeches, the ceremonies, the crowds. Ahead, the vast emptiness of the Arctic. It was the last time, Peary knew, that he would ever feel the strange thrill of heading for the unknown. He was fifty-two years old—really too old already and certainly too old to try again. He must make it now or never.

IV   NORTH TO CAPE SHERIDAN

A crash of crockery woke up Donald Mac-Millan in the tiny cabin he shared with George Borup on the *Roosevelt*. They had been steaming north now for ten days, but this was the first time in rough waters—the night they left Sydney, Nova Scotia, traditional jumping-off place for all Arctic explorers.

The *Roosevelt* was rolling wildly. Her rounded bottom, so well designed for withstanding the ice, was never meant for heavy seas. Canteens, snowshoes, rifles, knives, cameras—all the things an explorer needs in the Arctic—were clattering and tumbling about the room. Water sloshed around the floor, adding to the mess. Borup, who had never been at sea before, gasped as the cabin lamp literally jumped out of its bracket and landed upside down in the water pitcher.

On north the *Roosevelt* creaked and wallowed, through the Straits of Belle Isle, by the lonely lighthouse at Point Amour. She was edging up the coast of Labrador now. July 20, she sighted her first iceberg . . . later that day she stopped at Cape St. Charles, a lonely little whaling station. Here she picked up 17,000 pounds of whale meat —food for the Eskimo dogs that would pull the sledges.

July 21, the ship slipped into Hawke Harbor, still farther up the Labrador coast. Here she joined the steamer *Erik,* chartered by the Peary Arctic Club as an extra supply boat. The *Erik* was loaded with coal and twenty-five more tons of whale meat. She also carried three paying passengers—the young New Haven millionaire Harry Whitney and his friends Walter Larned and George Norton. They had nothing to do with the expedition; they simply craved excitement and some big-game hunting. Peary had worries enough without taking on passengers, yet they were will-ing to pay $1,500 apiece, and he needed every cent he could get. At the moment, as they sat among the rotting whale blubber, they must have wondered whether the cruise was worth the price.

As the two reeking ships lay at anchor together, a dainty white vessel steamed unexpectedly into the harbor. This was the Harkness yacht *Wakiva*. She was far from home, but with so much inter-est in polar exploration it had become fashionable for American millionaires to cruise the north-ern waters. True, they never saw the real Arctic —or even a polar bear—but there were occasional icebergs, the barren coast, the screaming gulls, the mysterious long twilights of the midnight sun.

But no one had bargained for this. These two black, foul-smelling ships were impossible. Yet it was too late to turn back without causing offense, so Mr. Harkness and his guests, including several ladies in fluffy white dresses, paid a cour-tesy call. The men on the *Roosevelt* did their best to rise to the occasion. From the rail to Peary's cabin they laid a plank across the mass of jelly-like blubber. The ladies paled but made it, and no one in either group ever mentioned the incredible smell. It was perhaps an all-time high in good manners.

On to Turnavik still farther up the coast. Here on July 22 Peary picked up fifty pairs of sealskin boots from Captain Bob Bartlett's father, who ran the local trading station. Now at last the *Roosevelt* headed northeast for Greenland.

A grinding crash shook George Borup the first

Except for the Eskimos, the deck of the *Roosevelt* must have looked very much like this when Harry Harkness and his party visited the ship at Hawke Harbor. Here, on the deck strewn with rotting blubber, Eskimos butcher one of the walruses shot by Peary's men on the way to Etah. Note the sign, "Positively No Admittance," outside Peary's cabin.

afternoon out. He dashed from his cabin, half expecting to find the *Roosevelt* aground. To his delight the ship was merely pushing aside her first ice. July 26, and she crossed the Arctic Circle. They were really far north now—ice floes, bergs, occasional seals. There was also daylight all the time, for in the Arctic summer it is always light, just as in winter it is always dark.

As they steamed on, the men worked at sorting out the supplies that cluttered the ship. The main deck remained a mass of whale meat and howling Eskimo dogs. Below, conditions were even worse. In the rear hold Borup tried to help MacMillan sort a jumble of canned goods: jam, beans, soup, everything that might be needed for two years in the wilderness. At last one morning the rolling ship and reeking whale meat proved too much for Borup. He bolted on deck and headed for the rail. Peary turned out to be as thoughtful as ever when his men were in trouble. He gently held out his favorite cure for seasickness—a glass of champagne and a couple of crackers.

July 30, and the great glistening peaks of Greenland loomed into view. Off Bushnan Island the

Roosevelt veered west along the coast toward a rocky headland called Cape York. As the little ship poked through the ice, Peary spied a couple of Eskimo tents nestled on a hill. Captain Bartlett sounded the whistle.

The bleak coast echoed with the sound. Auks, gulls whirled in excitement. Then from the tents burst a dozen little fur-clad figures, happily swarming to the shore. For the Smith Sound Eskimos this was the great day—"Peary-aksoah" had returned.

It was quite a reunion. The Eskimos were delighted to see Peary again. For eighteen years he had lived among this gentle tribe that roamed the coast from here to Etah, a tiny settlement two hundred miles farther north. He nursed them, fed them, gave them guns, knives, and lamps. In return they gladly clothed him, hunted for him, provided his dogs, handled the sledges, and were willing to follow him literally to the end of the world.

By now Peary knew them all. He knew exactly who were the best sledge drivers, who had the best dogs, who had the courage for the long dangerous

Seegloo (right), shown here at Fort Conger, was twenty-four in 1908 and the finest sledge driver among the Eskimos. He first showed his indomitable spirit when his group got lost returning from Peary's 1906 attempt. Seegloo refused to face starvation, was found hunting with a bow and arrow fashioned from a snowshoe and a spoon.

trip across the sea ice. He even knew who had the wives who could sew the best—important, for the women and children came along to stitch the furs and boots.

His eye fell on Seegloo. Here was an old campaigner, a tower of strength on the unsuccessful

1906 attempt. But he had almost starved to death that time, barely made it back to Greenland. Would he risk it again? Of course he would. The hardware he would get if they reached "the Big Nail" would make him a millionaire, by Eskimo standards, for the rest of his life.

Peary selected a few more recruits; then the *Roosevelt* and *Erik* headed north from Cape York on August 1. In and out of ice-packed coves the two ships dipped, picking up more Eskimos and dogs. Soon Kudlooktoo joined them—he was the only Eskimo who had bothered to learn English. Farther up the coast they added "Harrigan"—he understood no English but knew all the words to the song he was named after.

At North Star Bay Ooqueah joined the party. He was in love with the tribal patriarch's daughter, but the old man thought he was too poor. A year with Peary would fix that. The whale boat Peary had promised anyone who reached the Pole should make him irresistible.

But Ooqueah wasn't all that Peary found at North Star Bay. In a native tent he came across an ordinary American trunk. It was marked simply "F. A. Cook, Brooklyn, N. Y." The doctor, the Eskimos vaguely explained, had passed through the previous year. Was he really still bound for the Pole too?

Well, no time to worry about that. Peary had too much to do before winter set in and the long continuous Arctic night began. He must find still more Eskimos and dogs. He must start the work of building sledges and sewing the clothes. Above all he must find food. Unlike earlier explorers, Peary did not depend only on canned goods—he knew that lack of fresh food often caused scurvy. So he looked to the fresh meat found in the Arctic itself—foxes, hares, polar bears, seals, musk oxen, and especially walrus meat for the dogs.

Ooqueah, twenty years old, was "childlike and bland," according to Henson. But no one had stronger motives for going to the Pole, for he hoped to win his bride with the guns and hardware promised by Peary. Ooqueah's girl was the daughter of the tribal patriarch, who had been the first Eskimo to be hired on Peary's initial expedition to the Arctic.

Courtesy of The Explorers Club, New York City

A crash of rifle fire shook the icy stillness on August 5 as Borup, MacMillan, and several Eskimos took off in a whale boat after some walruses dozing on an ice cake. It was no picnic—like shooting musk oxen. Those clumsy animals just formed a tight circle, heads turned to the attackers. But walruses were dangerous. They traveled in large herds, usually fought together, and were always mean and tricky. This time an old bull walrus almost rammed the whale boat.

The Eskimos screamed and thrashed at him with oars and boathooks. Borup and MacMillan poured in gunfire. In the nick of time they managed to shoot and harpoon him. Hard work, but 1,500 more pounds of meat were added to the larder.

Steaming on, the *Roosevelt* at last reached Etah on August 7. Here she was joined by the *Erik*, and for the next week the two little ships lay side by side while the *Roosevelt* made ready for the final push north. This was the last chance to take stock—the northernmost settlement in the world. At that there were only a few Eskimo families here, but the harbor was perfect—an ink-blue fjord cut deep into rugged hills that were splashed with orange lichen. Strangely beautiful surroundings for the dirty job at hand. The *Roosevelt*'s men sweated through the twenty-four-hour daylight . . . cleaning the furnaces, restowing cargo, shifting fifty tons of whale meat from the *Erik,* plus some three hundred tons of coal. Another fifty tons of coal were stored on the shore— it would be a godsend on the trip back.

The men were still toiling away one morning when an American dory suddenly appeared from

This photograph, taken from the supply ship *Erik,* shows the *Roosevelt* as it lay at anchor in Etah harbor. Here preparations were made for the last, most difficult part of the ship's course, the journey to Cape Sheridan. The vessel was washed, the boilers were scoured and filled with fresh water, the furnaces were cleaned, and the cargo was shifted.

the north. A ragged, frantic figure pulled at the oars. This turned out to be Rudolph Francke, Dr. Cook's only white companion the previous winter. Cook had left him in charge of some supplies at Anoratok several miles up the coast, but it had been a dreadful year for Francke. Hating walrus meat, he tried living off canned goods; now he was half starved and racked with scurvy. He begged Peary to let him go back on the *Erik*.

The commander agreed, but he was none too happy about it. After all, this unexpected passenger was inherited from a rival who boasted he would get to the Pole first himself . . . a man who even now was somewhere to the northwest.

August 15, snow began falling. It was a harbinger of winter—time to push on before the sea froze, blocking the way completely. Three days later the *Roosevelt* cast off and slowly headed north in a driving sleet storm.

Behind lay the *Erik*, now stripped of supplies and riding high on the water. The little ship had done her job. Soon she would head back for New York with a skeleton crew and two of the millionaire sportsmen. The third, Harry Whitney, stayed on to hunt polar bears. As the ships parted the

Erik gave three long whistle blasts of farewell. The *Roosevelt* answered and her last link with civilization was gone.

Ahead lay 350 miles of trouble—the long ice-jammed passage that led north between Greenland and Ellesmere Island. First she must pass through Kane Basin, then the Kennedy and Robeson channels. But whatever the name, it was all dangerous. Treacherous tides and currents churned the waters; constantly shifting ice might crush the vessel anytime. Only four ships had ever made it through here, and the *Roosevelt* herself was almost crushed in 1906. Yet if she could fight her way to Cape Sheridan, the prize would be well worth the risk. She would then be at the edge of the Arctic Ocean . . . less than five hundred miles from Peary's dream, the Pole itself.

Turning into Kane Basin, the *Roosevelt* certainly didn't look like a ship on such a dangerous mission. She looked much more like a slovenly excursion boat. Her decks seethed with the laughing, yelling Eskimos—forty-nine altogether. They were everywhere—exploring the cabins, playing practical jokes, trying out mysterious new kinds of food like biscuits and sugar, examining such miracles as watches and fountain pens. There was only one place they weren't allowed to go. On the door of Peary's cabin was a large sign that said "Positively No Admittance." No Eskimo knew how to read, but every one of them knew exactly what it meant.

The *Roosevelt* steamed on, looking more and

Commander Peary distributes utensils to Eskimo women who sewed fur clothing for him and his men, and whose husbands served on the expedition. Peary gave this tribe of Eskimos medical supplies and superior hunting weapons, but felt that further exposure to civilization could only harm them.

more a shambles. Besides the Eskimos there were 246 dogs in the waist of the ship—all yelping in a furious free-for-all. The quarterdeck smelled worse than ever with 70 tons of whale meat and the blubber of 50 very dead walruses. First evening out Captain Bob Bartlett had peaches for dessert. He ate them all right, but the smell was so awful he couldn't even taste them.

Soon the ship was deep in the ice. Great bergs slid by, often just missing the hull. Flat masses of shifting ice closed and parted . . . sometimes leaving just enough room to slip through, other times blocking the way altogether.

High on the mast Captain Bartlett swung in a barrel, shouting orders through a megaphone to the helmsman below. Sometimes he would try to dodge the ice. Sometimes he would try to pry it apart, using the ship's strong steel prow as a crowbar. Sometimes he would simply try to smash his way through. Then the *Roosevelt* would hurtle forward, hit the ice with a great crash, back astern, then hurtle forward again. From his perch on the mast, Bartlett would root her on as though she were alive: "Rip 'em, Teddy, bite 'em in two! That's fine, my beauty! Now—again!"

From the crow's nest one-hundred feet above the deck, Captain Bartlett bellowed orders to the men below to guide the *Roosevelt* through the ice-choked Kennedy and Robeson channels. As the right-left blows of the prow separated huge cakes of ice, this mast would, according to George Borup, "swing back and forth like a bamboo in a simoon."

Mile after mile, day after day, the ship fought her way north. But sometimes all Bartlett's magic didn't work, and the *Roosevelt* would be caught for hours in a floe. Then the ice would press against her sides, crushing her, squeezing her, putting her in deadly danger. August 29 was such a day, but it was hard to believe it. The ship was draped in flags, and Peary broke open a bottle of champagne. It was Robert E. Peary, Jr.'s fifth birthday.

They were still frozen fast on the 31st, and Donald MacMillan could stand it no longer. Bursting with animal energy, he took off for the shore and raced aimlessly over the hills and rocks. He had no hat, no coat, no protection at all, and since it was $17°$ below, he inevitably came down with a high fever the following day. Peary could have lectured him, but with the gentleness he always mustered when his men were really down, he said nothing. Instead, every evening he sat at the pianola and pumped out MacMillan's favorite song, "The Wedding of the Winds."

Finally they began moving again. Lying in his bunk, MacMillan once again heard the reassuring sounds of the *Roosevelt*'s engines, the laughing

Eskimos, the crunch of the ship fighting through ice. Then on September 5 the noise stopped, and George Borup yelled through the cabin door, "We're there, Mac!"

MacMillan was still too weak to care where, but a new set of sounds gave him the answer. The clanking of winches, the scramble of feet down the side of the ship, the barking of dogs ashore—all told him that the *Roosevelt* had finally arrived at Cape Sheridan. She was the farthest north a ship had ever steamed. The first big step to the Pole had been won.

V   THE LONG WINTER NIGHT

George Borup raced madly after his dog team. He had been at Cape Sheridan two weeks now—working with his dog sledge most of the time—and felt he was getting to be quite an expert. But it turned out that the dogs didn't agree. The first time he halted to untangle the traces, they took off the instant he loosened his grip.

He finally managed to collar two or three, but the rest ran the six miles back to the *Roosevelt* alone. Hours later Borup himself appeared as the Eskimos hooted and howled with laughter. He had learned the hard way that an Arctic sledge driver's greatest humiliation is to lose his own dog team.

Gradually he learned other things too about handling a sledge. To turn right, he must give the Eskimo command *how-eh!* To go left, it was *ash-oo!* Straight ahead meant *huk, huk, huk!* And he also discovered that if he yelled at the dogs in English, they just sat down and looked around in surprise.

He spent hours practicing with the 25-foot whip the Eskimos used. They could flick any particular dog in a team, but Borup usually missed altogether—or ended up stinging himself. He learned to feed the dogs too, and to rest them without snarling the traces. The secret was to stake the team out around a central post stuck in the snow, but this was easier said than done. The dogs seemed to know an infinite number of ways to get tangled up.

But finally he mastered the art. Then nothing could compare with the sheer thrill of guiding a sledge as it skimmed across the ice. The dogs were harnessed fanwise—usually eight to a team— and they barked and yelped with excitement as they raced along. The driver ran behind, shouting them on, cracking his whip, feeling the strange comradeship that always evolves when man and dog are together.

These runs were far more than practice jaunts. Peary had decided to make Cape Columbia, ninety miles farther west, his jump-off point for the polar dash next spring. This would offset an easterly ice-drift, making the return trip from the Pole much shorter. But it also meant hard work now—shifting tons of supplies to the new advance base before the long winter night set in.

The first party set out September 16 to deposit supplies along the route. On September 28 another took a load all the way to Cape Columbia. All through October the work continued. Sometimes it was easy—the sledges just glided along; but often it took every ounce of strength to guide a team over the rough, tumbling coastal ice.

With trips like these George Borup soon became an expert sledge driver indeed. And so did Donald MacMillan and Dr. Goodsell, the other two "tenderfeet," as the newcomers were usually called. But there was always so much more to learn— boots were drier with a little grass inside . . . pants should be polar-bear skin, the only fur that stayed warm, wet or dry . . . long woolen underwear soaked up too much moisture, merely made a man feel colder.

The new men watched in awe as the Eskimos showed them how to build an igloo. The natives laid the blocks of snow not on top of each other but in a spiral going counter-clockwise. Working together, three men took only an hour to build a house eight feet in diameter and eight feet high.

The entrance to the igloo was just big enough to squeeze through; it could then be shut with another snow block. Inside there was room for three men, who slept together on a snow platform opposite the entrance. Even here there were special tricks to learn: the higher the sleeping platform, the warmer the air. If it was $50°$ below outside, in the shelter of a well-made igloo the temperature would be—only $40°$ below.

And so the days passed, while all the time it got darker and colder. The long Arctic winter was approaching now, and the sun was moving south. October 12, it slipped below the horizon. November 5, even the light was gone. There could be no more heavy supply trips to Cape Columbia this year.

When the *Roosevelt* was safely moored at Cape Sheridan and the supplies were unloaded, Peary ordered the start of the autumn sledging. One purpose was to train the "tenderfeet"; another was to carry supplies to points along the route to Cape Columbia, the jumping-off place

for the Pole. This photograph, taken on September 16, 1908, shows Ross Marvin, Dr. Goodsell, George Borup, and eleven Eskimos, setting out on a trip with fourteen sledge loads. When the big day finally came, the main party leaving Cape Columbia for the Pole looked like this.

But the men kept as busy as ever. In the old days Arctic explorers did nothing during the long months of darkness. Often they simply worried the winter away. Peary changed all that. When the moon was out, parties were off hunting, fishing, studying the rise and fall of the tides. When there was no moon, they had plenty to do around the ship—making sledges, sorting provisions, humoring the Eskimo women who sewed their furs.

Peary was busiest of all, constantly studying new ways to save weight and time. He taught the men to use their hooded *kooletahs* instead of sleeping bags . . . saving sixteen pounds on every sledge. He invented an alcohol stove that boiled water in only ten minutes—that would save nearly an hour a day in making tea. He made the Eskimo sledge more maneuverable by lengthening it to twelve feet and rounding off the ends—that should save time too . . . maybe the difference between victory and defeat.

Mid-November found him wrestling with a brand-new problem. The dogs suddenly began dying. If this continued there was no point in thinking up clever new ways to save a pound or a minute. They couldn't go anywhere without their sledges. Yet the pack kept shrinking—to 193 on November 8 . . . to 188 on the 10th . . . to only 160 on the 25th. Desperately Peary juggled the diet, traced the trouble to rotten whale meat. He switched to walrus and the crisis was over.

Thanksgiving, and the men were off again on various assignments. Measuring the tide at Cape Columbia, Donald MacMillan decided to give his Eskimos a taste of New England tradition. He would make them a cranberry pie. He had a jar of cranberries to start with, but the crust was another matter. Finally he made "flour" by pounding some crackers to dust, and for "shortening"—well, that tin of musk ox tallow would do. The Eskimos politely expressed their appreciation, and MacMillan considered his holiday treat a great success . . . even after he discovered the "shortening" was not musk-ox tallow after all but Dr. Goodsell's favorite remedy for frozen feet, a can of boric-acid salve.

December 21 saw a far bigger celebration. For this was the winter solstice—when the sun reached its farthest point south and started north again. After months of ever-growing darkness, it was the most important day in the year for an Arctic explorer. At 4 P.M. Peary assembled the Eskimos on the *Roosevelt*'s deck. Pulling out his watch, he declared that even now the sun was heading back. Marvin excitedly clanged the ship's bell . . . Henson fired his revolver . . . and Borup set off a blast of photo-flashlight powder. It was such a dramatic ceremony that one Eskimo dashed south over the ice to meet the returning sun.

Christmas was like Christmas everywhere when men are away from home. Lots of good cheer, but just a touch of loneliness too. It was a time for letters carefully saved, for presents that had waited long unopened. Later there were sports, prizes, a giant feast, and even a track meet for the Eskimos.

In comparison New Year's Eve seemed quite tame—but it was hard to give 1909 a proper celebration when the temperature stood at 48° below.

January passed . . . then into February, and one morning George Borup noticed a strong reddish tinge along the southern horizon. Nobody needed to tell him what it meant. With a burst of joy he gave his college cheer for the returning sun. It was not above the horizon—there would still be weeks of twilight before it actually reappeared—but at least there was light again.

Clearly it was nearly time to start. Henson gave the sledges a last check . . . Marvin packed his instruments . . . Borup and MacMillan gave each other crew cuts. The Eskimos grew more and more excited—and worried too. More than one began to have second thoughts about the long trip across the ice of the polar sea. It would be quite different from sledging along the coast, where the ice might be rough but was always steady as the land itself.

That sea ice moved. No matter how cold the weather—no matter how thick the ice—the tides and currents were always at work. They slammed floes together, piling up huge pressure ridges . . . or pulled them apart, leaving ugly dark leads of water that could swallow up a man forever.

Peary sensed the Eskimos' restlessness. On February 14 he called them together and showed them once again the prizes they would get, once the goal was reached. He brought out the rifles and knives, he pointed to the sturdy whaleboats.

Photograph by Robert E. Peary © Robert E. Peary, Jr., and Marie Peary Stafford, courtesy National Geographic Society

Peary and his men often had to cross pressure ridges like this one, some of them over sixty feet high. Getting over them required brute strength. Dogs usually had to be whipped before they would follow. Peary said that the weight of the fully loaded sledges "sometimes seemed likely to tear the muscles from one's shoulder blades."

Dark eyes lit with excitement . . . confidence returned . . . the crisis passed.

Next day, February 15, the first members of the polar party started off for Cape Columbia. Once again the sledges bounced and glided over that well-traveled trail. There were many more hours of daylight now, and the way was easy to see. The men pushed ahead with mounting excitement. This time was different from those long supply trips during the fall. This time they wouldn't be coming back until the Pole was won or lost.

By late February they were all at the Cape. Peary, his six assistants, and seventeen Eskimos huddled in a bleak community of igloos bravely christened Crane City. The supplies were stacked in neat piles, the nineteen sledges in good repair. There had been no more trouble with the dogs; 133 were on hand in excellent shape—easily enough for the trip.

February 27, the day before starting out, they loaded the sledges. Again Peary proved a master of detail. He had worked out to the last ounce how much food a man or a dog would need a day. Each man required a pound of biscuit, a pound of pemmican, four ounces of condensed milk, half an ounce of tea. The dogs could get along with less: a pound of pemmican a day.

Now to load the sledges. Again that same meticulous care: 500 pounds of "dog" pemmican in red tins on the bottom . . . the 50 pounds of "man" pemmican in blue tins . . . then cans of milk, tea, and alcohol . . . then rifles, snowshoes, boots, tools, all covered by a small fur rug. It added up to a compact 650-pound load—as much as the men could handle when there was any lifting to be done.

Packed this way, each of the supporting divisions was self-sufficient. In fact each team was self-sufficient except for a stove. There was only one of these for every two sledges, so if anything happened to that, those depending on it simply had to double up with some other unit or go cold. Otherwise even if some of the party got separated from the rest, they had enough rations to keep going for fifty or sixty days. If they weren't back by then, they would never be back. No one returned from the polar sea ice after the spring thaw at the end of April.

Sledges loaded, the men gathered that night in

Peary's igloo for last instructions. This time the commander gave no technical advice; the time was past for that. Instead he spoke words from the heart. He said he had always believed in action—not hot air. He told them the next weeks would be "undiluted hell"—but other brave men had come through worse. He played on their emotions like a skillful coach, reminding Borup of "the way a football team gathers round its leader just before trotting out on the field for a big game."

Late that evening Marvin, MacMillan, and Borup slipped into Bartlett's igloo for a smaller, more intimate session. Over the months these four men had become intensely devoted to each other, and this last night called for something special. First they sang their college songs. Next they all joined hands, and each man led his own college cheer. Then they quietly pledged themselves to give their all for Peary, and shaking hands, they joined in one last song of friendship.

Sunday, February 28, dawned clear, calm, and 50° below. As soon as it was light, Captain Bob Bartlett started north over the frozen Arctic Ocean with three Eskimos and a single sledge. As he shoved off Peary ran beside him for a hundred yards or so, shouting last-second instructions.

The plan was for Bartlett to lead the way. He would pioneer the trail . . . hack a path through the tumbling, jagged offshore ice, camping about ten miles out. The others would start later—first Borup, then everyone else the following morning. The main party would trace Bartlett's course and use his igloos at night. Meanwhile the captain would be trail-blazing the next day's march. He would keep ahead of them until he wore out; then his place would be taken by somebody else.

Two hours later George Borup started off in Bartlett's tracks. He commanded four sledges, driven by three Eskimos and himself. They were to overtake Bartlett, stick with him for three days, then stockpile their supplies and return to Cape Columbia for more.

As Borup set out, Peary ran alongside him too, pouring out more bits of final advice. Borup told him not to worry—this was his sister's birthday and she always brought him luck.

At 6:30 the following morning, March 1, the fourteen sledges of the main party stood ready to follow. They were in single file, with Henson's party in the lead. After all these years with Peary, he could pick up Bartlett's trail if anyone could. Then came Marvin, MacMillan, and Goodsell's divisions. Together with Borup and later Bartlett, they were the "supporting parties." Each had the job of keeping Peary's unit fed for five days . . . then back to Cape Columbia, ultimately leaving the commander to carry on alone.

Everyone in place, Peary now moved to the very rear. Here he could keep an eye on things ahead, help with repairs, stop any straggling. Quickly he gave one last glance at the sky. Instead of the crystal calm of the previous day, a biting wind now howled from the east. It could bury Bartlett's trail with drifting snow. It could open new, deadly leads in the sea ice. It could shatter the men's strength. It could, in short, wreck all his plans and hopes.

But there was no turning back. In a clear loud voice that could be heard even above the screeching wind, Peary shouted the order that launched the men on their way: "Forward, march!"

His crisp command was perhaps not so much the beginning of his greatest drive on the Pole, as it was an end to the beginning. For it was now clear that everything in the past was part of his preparation: The schoolboy hikes that developed his stamina . . . the engineering projects that trained his mind . . . the voyage to Nicaragua that whetted his wanderlust . . . the first trip to Greenland that kindled his yearning for the Pole. And all those Arctic trips over the next twenty-two years were but preparation too—the defeats, the heartbreaks, the discoveries. Even the smallest things, like learning that a sledge-driver needs half an ounce of tea a day. Yes, it was all part of the beginning; now would come the test.

VI   OUT OVER THE SEA ICE

Commander Peary stared into the haze in startled disbelief. They had been pushing north for only a few hours, yet here was one of the Eskimos already heading back. It was Kyutah from Marvin's group—he had smashed his sledge and was returning to Cape Columbia for a spare. Peary simply told him to hurry—catch up as soon as he could.

Within an hour another Eskimo, Kudlooktoo, also appeared, heading south. He too had wrecked his sledge and wanted another. It was too much. Peary chewed him out unmercifully. When it came to interfering with his life's dream, the commander was no longer the Eskimo's kindly guardian. He was a hard, tough master, capable of brutal words and decisions. The tirade over, Kudlooktoo continued on back, sullen and abashed.

Peary pressed on. He had now left the fringe of glacial ice bordering the shore, was starting across the frozen Arctic Ocean itself. The first few miles proved a nightmare. The moving sea ice, pressing against the immovable shore ice, piled up a huge mass of tumbling blocks and pressure ridges. A few miles of this and it was easy to see why the Eskimos ahead had found so much trouble.

The men painfully chipped at the ice spurs that barred every path. They skidded over occasional stretches as slippery as a ballroom floor. They wrestled the sledges through impossible crevices, up impossible hummocks, over impossible ridges. As the drivers heaved and tugged and sweated away, all too often the dogs simply sat wagging their tails, enjoying the sight of men working so hard.

Finally they emerged onto the relatively smooth ice of the old floes. The Arctic still had plenty of perils to offer, but at least this zone of crazy, tumbling ice was past. Gratefully, the men reached Bartlett's first camp ten miles out and collapsed in relief for the night.

Peary was just settling down when one of Henson's Eskimos burst into the igloo. Eyes bulging with fright, he jabbered that evil spirits were in camp—the stove wouldn't work. The last part, at least, was true. At $50°$ below it was so cold the alcohol wouldn't vaporize enough for a match to light it directly. Peary solved the problem by first dropping a strip of burning paper into the alcohol.

At 6:30 next morning they were on their way again. It was easier going now but still none too smooth—MacMillan upset his sledge three times. About 4 P.M. they sighted a low, gray cloud directly ahead, and Peary's heart sank. A cloud like that always meant open water.

Sure enough, within minutes they ran into their first lead—an ugly black ribbon of water that cut squarely across the trail. It had formed some time since Bartlett and Borup passed the day before, but already it was four hundred yards wide. There was nothing to do but camp for the

Photograph by Robert E. Peary © Robert E. Peary, Jr., and Marie Peary Stafford, courtesy National Geographic S[...]

On April 6, 1909, Peary made his last long forced march, between $89° 25'$ and $89° 57'$. During the halt for lunch this picture was taken, showing (left to right) Henson, Egingwah, Ootah, Seegloo, and Ooqueah. Between Egingwah and Ootah are two of Peary's specially made alcohol stoves, each of which could boil a gallon of water in ten minutes at $-50°$.

night, hoping that the ice would soon freeze over or the bitter wind would drive it together again. Putting the delay to good use, MacMillan dropped a line through a hole to see how deep the water was.

78

Suddenly he broke through the thin ice. Marvin hauled him out, but there he stood—a sopping bundle of fur at $40°$ below. He raced back to camp to find Peary already waiting with a dry change of clothes. Then yanking off the ice-coated boots, the commander warmed MacMillan's freezing feet against his own bare chest. Peary would still do anything for the men who backed him up.

Next morning the lead closed, and they started off again. Racing over the undulating young ice that now covered the lead, the men stopped with a jolt on the other side. There was no longer any sign of the trail. The far "shore" of the lead had drifted sideways during the night, carrying the trail with it—but no one could tell how far or whether to the right or left. Kyutah, the best trail finder among the Eskimos, finally picked it up over a mile to the west.

Pounding on, it was late that afternoon when another sharp-eyed Eskimo suddenly noticed footprints heading the opposite way. Clearly Borup, going back for his second load, had already passed. He had missed connections due to the break in the trail.

It was a heavy blow for Peary. He had counted on meeting Borup. He wanted to tell him that the alcohol tins were leaking badly and an extra supply was desperately needed—something Borup couldn't hope to know without being told.

Only one thing to do. Peary quickly ordered Ross Marvin and Kyutah to put down their loads, hustle back to Cape Columbia, and fill in Borup on the problem. This done, the rest of the party hurried on.

Thursday, March 4, brought more trouble. It was oppressively warm—the temperature stood at a sultry 9° below—and leads soon formed on all sides. For a while the men managed to dodge them, but their luck ran out late that afternoon. They were about forty-five miles from Cape Columbia when they came to a harrowing stretch of open water—so broad they christened it the "Big Lead."

Here they caught up with Bartlett. He had already been held up for twenty-four hours, and the lead still showed no signs of closing. There was nothing to do but camp and wait.

March 5 . . . 6 . . . 7 passed and still no sign

that the lead would close. Dr. Goodsell restlessly flipped the pages of a little book of Shakespeare he had tucked among his things. Henson tried to study his Bible. MacMillan morosely examined a frostbitten heel—it was definitely beginning to go bad. The party had only one consolation: on March 5 the days of just twilight came to an end, and the sun at last reappeared from the south.

It made little difference to Peary. Day after day he just paced and paced. Occasionally he looked south, hoping at least for some sign of Borup and Marvin. Other times he simply studied the northern horizon, wondering whether once again the defenses of the Arctic were going to turn him back.

The Eskimos gradually became restless. Talking among themselves, they remembered last time . . . when they almost starved. They recalled how the leads had opened up, trapping them for days. They knew it could happen again.

MacMillan desperately tried to buck them up. He told his best jokes, walked on his hands, and tried other stunts. Finally he even staged a track meet with all sorts of games—sprints, jumping, thumb wrestling. It helped but not enough. At last on March 7 Peary ordered the two chief grumblers, Pooadloonah and Panikpah, to go back to Cape Columbia. He gave them a note for Borup and Marvin—"Hurry, hurry!" Then he handed them a note for the *Roosevelt*. It was curt and to the point: Throw these Eskimos and their families off the ship.

Stiff punishment, for it meant expelling the Eskimos three hundred miles from home without food or equipment. But Peary was adamant. He would risk his life for a loyal companion, but woe to the man who threatened his last try for the Pole.

March 8 . . . 9 . . . 10, and still the lead stayed open. Peary continued to pace the days away, rarely saying anything. Occasionally he looked at Bartlett, who was doing a little pacing of his own. One glance at the captain's taut jaw showed that he too was full of grim thoughts.

Then, miraculously, on March 10 the lead began to freeze over. Fresh thin ice appeared, and by the 11th it was strong enough to cross. But now a new problem: Should they go on without waiting for Borup and Marvin? They were bringing the alcohol to light the stoves that meant hot tea.

If the party waited, they could be sure of their tea. If they went on, they might have to go without it—and tea was considered a "must" in the Arctic. For Peary the choice was easy: "I don't know how long a man can work and live at $50°$ and $60°$ below without a hot drink. I think we may find out. It's got to be done."

March 11, they were on their way again. The young ice that covered the lead was loose and flexible—it was like walking on thin shingles—but the men raced across, spacing themselves so they would not put too much weight on any one spot.

Pushing on, they found smoother going. But for once, Peary's mind was on things that lay behind. Despite his brave words, he was desperately worried about Borup and Marvin. He could try to make it without tea, but in his heart he knew the chances would be slim indeed.

March 12 . . . 13, two more days of worry. And as if to underline the need for fuel, the temperature plunged to $59°$ below. It was so cold the men's beards froze stiff. Everyone was cold

There were three ways to cross open lanes of water. The simplest was to use one of Peary's extra-long sledges as a bridge. Another was to have two men jump across a rapidly widening lead and toss a rope to them; the remaining men would cut a cake of ice with their pickaxes and use it as a ferry boat on which to pull the dogs, sledges, and themselves across the lead, as shown above.

he third method was planned for the return trip, when warmer pring weather might keep the widest leads from refreezing. If this appened, Peary expected to use an ingenious system of sealskin floats. wo sledges would be lashed together, with floats placed underneath; he resulting raft would be floated across the lead, with snowshoes or edge crossbars used as paddles. Fortunately the ice held firm, and 'eary's men never had to use this method.

and depressed when the commander finally ended the day's march and ordered them to start building their igloos.

"Kling-mik-sue!   Kling-mik-sue!" suddenly shrieked an Eskimo who had climbed an ice hummock to look around. Even the newcomers knew this meant "Dogs are coming!" All rushed to see where the man was pointing. There on the southern horizon hung a thin silvery mist—the steam of dogs breathing into the cold Arctic air. It was always the first sign that a team was approaching.

Marvin? Borup? All eyes strained southward. No, it turned out to be Seegloo, one of Borup's Eskimos. Breathlessly he stumbled into camp, gasped that Marvin and Borup were on their way. They too had been held up by leads but were making double marches to catch up. They had sent Seegloo ahead to reassure Peary that his supplies were coming. His feat in overtaking the main party was perhaps the greatest in all the history of dog sledging—with less than four hours' sleep he had covered 74 miles in eighteen hours.

Peary nearly collapsed in relief and that night

slept like a child. All next day, the 14th, the party stayed in camp, waiting for Borup and Marvin to come. Toward evening, they again saw the telltale mist on the horizon. Minutes later Marvin pounded into camp, closely followed by Borup.

They were full of stories of their adventures. Nearly everything had happened to them. Once even their igloo had caught fire—a strange thing for a house of snow to do. But it had been weatherproofed with canvas, and they had left the stove too close to that. No wonder their Eskimos were sure that evil spirits were loose and threatened to revolt. But everything had worked out in the end, and now they were all reunited.

But not for long. The time had come to start sending back the supporting parties. That day Peary had already despatched Dr. Goodsell with two sick Eskimos and twelve poor dogs. Now he told Donald MacMillan that he must go too. MacMillan's frostbitten heel had grown much worse, and if he stayed any longer he would only slow down everyone.

MacMillan was crushed. He had hoped to go

much farther north. But like all the others, he knew there was no arguing with Peary when the Pole was at stake.

He had one last night of old songs with Marvin, Borup, and Bartlett; then on the morning of March 15 he began trudging back south. Oddly enough almost the saddest moment was saying good-bye to his dogs. MacMillan had grown immensely fond of them and knew all too well that in sledge travel the toll would be high. He was right. When he ultimately had a chance to see them again, only two were left alive.

The main party hurried on—now down to sixteen men, twelve sledges, one hundred dogs. It was a day of bad leads, ominous rumbling and crumbling of ice. Frightening cracks and holes would appear unexpectedly as the men rushed across. Once two of Borup's dogs fell through a hole. Racing forward, he barely managed to stop the sledge from following; then with a giant effort he yanked out both dogs. They weighed about eighty pounds apiece, but Borup proved once again that in a real emergency a man can do amazing feats of strength with one hand.

March 16 . . . 17, they slogged on. Marvin

was now pioneering, the rest following about a day behind. The sun was higher, but it seemed colder than ever—again beards grew stiff and the medicinal brandy froze solid.

Two more days, and they were almost numb with weariness. In the endless, desolate waste their eyes began to play all sorts of strange tricks. An empty can of pemmican on the trail looked like a distant dog team; a dropped mitten looked like some unearthly animal.

March 20, and it was time for Borup to take the next supporting party back. Peary had tried to explain that every five days another group would return—but it was always hard when the moment came. Peary sensed it, and did his best to cheer up Borup by walking a little way with him on the homeward trail.

Then the men pushed on, with Bartlett again pioneering, Henson helping him, Marvin and Peary traveling a march behind. Day after day went by—and then on March 25 it was Marvin's turn to go back. As he started south with Kudlooktoo and "Harrigan," Peary called out a final word of advice, "Be careful of the leads, my boy!" Bartlett's words were more pointed: "I'll see you again in one of three places: heaven, hell, or the *Roosevelt!*" He never dreamed that it wouldn't be the *Roosevelt*.

Now Henson and Bartlett were the only assistants left. On they plodded, each hoping that the other would be the next sent back. It was like an Arctic version of "musical chairs" with the winner getting a chance to go with Peary all the way.

For a while Bartlett felt he might get the prize. He was clearly a fine pioneer, a natural born leader, a marvelously cool man in a pinch. And Peary certainly liked him. Yet Henson was indeed the better sledge driver. . . .

Peary being Peary, the choice was easy. Leaders were fine in civilization, and friends were a joy at home. But right now he was trying to get to the North Pole, and sledge driving was everything. He told Bartlett to be ready to start home on April 1.

The day dawned gray and cold. After rising, Bartlett trudged north alone for six more miles—he hoped at least to be the first person in history to cross the 88th parallel. As it turned out, he couldn't even have that satisfaction. When he got back to camp and took observations, he discovered that he had miscalculated the southerly drift of ice and missed his target by about six miles.

Parting with Peary, he was cheerful but disappointed. The commander understood perfectly but wasn't about to change his mind: "It's all in the game," he reminded the captain.

Bartlett knew, but still it was hard. He started south slowly, unconsciously hanging back in case some new summons might come from the north.

But Peary was no longer even thinking of him. All his attention was turned toward the Pole. As he later put it, "My work was still ahead, not in the rear."

VII   THE FINAL DASH

Robert E. Peary took a notch in his belt and started north again. It was shortly after midnight on the morning of April 2, and the Pole now lay 133 miles away. To reach it he had Henson, four Eskimos, five sledges, forty dogs.

They were the best of the lot. As planned, everyone else had gone back with the various supporting parties. Those left would follow him anywhere.

Henson had stood by him for eighteen years. Ootah, a great hunter, was considered the best all-around Eskimo in the tribe. His brother Egingwah had been loyal all through the darkest days of 1906. Seegloo had proved himself the greatest of sledge drivers when he overtook the main party to report that Borup and Marvin were coming. Young Ooqueah had achieved no such glory, but he too would go anywhere—he was already counting the rifles and knives that would win him the girl he wanted.

As they all pushed ahead, Peary for the first time was in the lead. He had been saving himself for precisely this moment. He wanted to be at his best for the final dash, when all his skill and experience would be needed. And now it was working just as he planned—he never felt stronger or more able to cope with any trouble.

He felt strangely young again. His mind drifted back to those early days in Greenland twenty-three years ago. This was just like them—the endless ice, the dazzling sun, the deep blue sky. Perhaps, he thought, a man always thinks of the start of his work when he feels it is nearing the end.

Spirits high, mile after mile he raced ahead. The ice was smooth, the weather calm, the sledging perfect. It seemed almost absurdly easy. After

Egingwah, aged twenty-six, weighed 175 pounds and was considered big for an Eskimo. Trapped by a lead in the ice on Peary's 1905–1906 expedition, he would have starved if he had not eaten his boots.

Courtesy of The Explorers Club, New York City

Ootah, Egingwah's brother, was thirty-four years old. A great hunter, a kind father, and a good provider, he was considered the best all-around member of the tribe. He too had been with Peary in 1905.

Courtesy of The Explorers Club, New York City

all these years—all these miles—had the Arctic finally run out of tricks?

No, it hadn't. Toward the end of the afternoon the men suddenly came to a lead just beginning to open. The gap was only ten yards wide, yet clearly too broad to jump. But a little way off they saw a place where the lead was filled with loose ice cakes.

Peary rushed to the spot, picked his way across from cake to cake, much the way a man might cross a stream by jumping from rock to rock. But these "rocks" were moving. The men constantly had to throw their weight this way or that to keep the cakes from tipping over.

It took even more skill to lure the dogs across and it was always hard to make them jump an opening crack. But an old trick worked in the end. A man would go ahead of his team and hold his hand out as though it held something good to eat. The ever-hungry sledge dogs always fell for that.

Safely across, Peary pushed on another mile. Then leaping over another small lead, he suddenly crashed through the ice and landed in water up to his hips. Fortunately, his waterproof trousers worked. He quickly crawled out, scraping off the ice as it formed on his fur. Ruefully he thought of the hot baths he used to take on the *Roosevelt*. The day's march was over now, and as the men built their igloos Peary totaled up the score. They had gone 25 miles in ten hours—the Pole now lay 108 miles ahead.

They were on their way again early on the 3rd. But today the ice was rougher and the going slower. Late in the afternoon Henson crashed through a stretch of thin ice. Floundering in deep water, he was yanked out just in time by Ootah.

Henson rushed ahead to Peary to describe his narrow escape. But the commander was in no mood to listen. He had just fallen in again himself.

All in all, a hard day—only 20 miles in ten hours. The Pole was still a good 88 miles off. Peary grimly took another hole in his belt.

A few hours' sleep and they were going again. They started off just before midnight on April 3, but this was not hard to do, for now it was always light. The sun and the moon both were up all the time—a gold and silver disc chasing each other around and around the sky.

Most of the 4th they kept traveling. They were speeding along now—trying to make up for lost time—and for once their luck held good. They hit a freshly frozen lead that ran north and south. It was like an avenue of polished ice, and Peary streaked north along the glistening surface. Ten hours of sledging, and he was less than 63 miles from the Pole.

It was the same story on April 5. More smooth ice and the party dashed 28 miles in ten hours. When they finally camped, they were only 35 miles from the goal.

They started off again before midnight on the 5th. This time Peary hoped to go the whole way— an all-out twelve-hour drive to the top of the world. Cracking their whips, shouting encouragement, the men stormed ahead. Even the dogs seemed to catch the spirit—they barked and yelped and bounded along.

The Eskimos were beside themselves. Normally they acted as though the Pole were a white man's whim; they themselves could take it or leave it.

But now they were wild with excitement. Dashing ahead, they scrambled to the top of every pressure ridge and searched the northern horizon, hoping to see "the Big Nail" itself.

At 10 A.M. on April 6 Peary finally ordered his men to halt and make camp. They were still on a waste of ice and snow—no different from anything else the past five weeks—but the commander seemed strangely satisfied. As the men unloaded the sledges, he carefully pulled a small package from under his *kooletah*. Lovingly he unfolded the old silk American flag he carried on every expedition. Mrs. Peary had given it to him fifteen years before, and he had left a piece of it at each of his "farthest norths." Now the flag was patched and discolored, but it still snapped in the breeze as he proudly planted it on his igloo.

"This, my boy," he told Henson, "is to be Camp Morris K. Jessup, the last and most northerly camp on earth." It seemed a fitting honor for Peary's greatest benefactor, for the commander was sure he had reached the North Pole at last. But when he adjusted his sextant for a noon observation, he discovered that he was at $89° \ 57'$—still three miles to go.

Three miles! They seemed more like three thousand just now. The last march had been a killer—32 miles in twelve hours—and Peary was completely exhausted. So with the goal actually in sight, he just couldn't take the last few steps. Instead he sank into his igloo. For the first time in his life he was too weary and numb to care.

It was different a few hours later. After a short nap those three miles looked like three feet. Grabbing his diary, he excitedly scribbled, "The Pole at last. The prize of three centuries. My dream and goal for twenty years. Mine at last! I cannot bring myself to realize it. It all seems so simple and commonplace."

At 6 P.M. he took a light sledge with two Eskimos and pushed on ten more miles. At midnight he took another set of observations. To his joy he was now *beyond* the Pole, heading south again.

A million thoughts danced through Peary's mind. What a remarkable sensation! In a march of a few hours he had passed from the western to the eastern hemisphere. He had traveled several miles north, then several miles south—all the while going in a straight line! East, west, and north had disappeared—there was only one direc-

At the Pole Peary took these four photographs. He turned his camera clockwise roughly ninety degrees after taking each picture, yet each one looks south. The view at the upper left faces toward Cape Columbia; if a man traveled south in this direction, he would eventually pass through Cape Cod. The picture at the upper right faces toward the Bering Strait, on the longitude passing through the middle of the Samoa Islands. The photograph at the lower left was taken looking toward Cape Chelyuskin, on the same longitude as Bangkok. The pic-

ture at the lower right looks toward Spitsbergen, which is on the longitude that passes close by Belgrade, Yugoslavia, and Warsaw, Poland. These photographs were made under the worst possible conditions. Temperatures were so low that the camera's mechanism often froze, and unless the cameraman remembered to hold his breath, it instantly made a coat of ice on the lens. When men removed their isinglass goggles to record their position or take photographs, the merciless glare caused severe headaches and even snowblindness for hours afterward.

tion, south. Every breeze that could possibly blow was southern. It was impossible to throw a snowball in any direction but south.

Back at Camp Jessup early on the 7th, Peary took still another set of observations. Then he was off with his sledge again. He spent most of the next thirty hours marching and countermarching over a ten-mile area. He took four different sets of observations—thirteen single altitudes of the sun—all putting him at or near the Pole. Overdoing it perhaps, but he wanted no arguments back home. No one must question his victory.

"We will plant the Stars and Stripes—at the North Pole," Peary announced when finally satisfied on the morning of April 7. Then he led Henson and the four Eskimos to a hummock not far from camp. It wasn't exactly the Pole, but it would do for a picture. He raised Mrs. Peary's flag and others too: the Navy League, the Red Cross, the D.A.R. peace emblem, the colors of his college fraternity, DKE.

Next he had Henson lead "three rousing cheers." The Eskimos were delighted to oblige. They were a little bewildered: This wasn't quite the way they imagined "the Big Nail," but they

On April 7, 1909, the five men who reached the North Pole with Peary posed for this picture. From left to right, Ooqueah holds the Navy League flag; Ootah, the flag of Peary's fraternity at Bowdoin College, Delta Kappa Epsilon; Henson, the Polar flag given Peary by his wife; Egingwah, the D.A.R. Peace Flag; and Seegloo, the Red Cross flag. The American flag was later planted on the ice mound in the background.

vaguely realized they were at the top of the world. More important, they knew that Peary had achieved his goal. They would get the promised hardware.

Now for the marker traditionally planted at the scene of every discovery. Peary used a glass bottle, cramming into it a diagonal strip of his flag and two separate statements, written just after his arrival the previous day. The first listed the members of the party; the second formally took possession of the North Pole "for and in the name of the President of the United States of America." In doing so, he was understandably proud though a little too enthusiastic, for in effect he was claiming a part of the ocean.

It was now almost time to start home—just one last thing to do. To Peary, who really loved his family and felt his greatest sacrifice was leaving them, it was perhaps his most important task. Taking an ordinary postcard from his gear, he scribbled a few hurried words to his wife; nothing remarkable, just the kind of card any lonely husband might send after a long, hard trip: "My dear Jo, I have won out at last. Have been here a day. I start for home and you in an hour. . . ."

VIII   THE RETURN

What a difference from the trip up, thought Matthew Henson. Then Peary never seemed to sleep, could hardly wait to plunge on after every stop. Now, as they started back on the afternoon of April 7, a violent reaction set in. His voice quavered, and after the first two marches south he was practically a dead weight. Most of the time he simply lay on top of his sledge.

Fortunately it didn't matter. The trail up was easy to follow going back. The igloos built on the way north were ready and waiting, whenever they needed rest. The weather was good, the ice quiet, the leads easy to cross. It seemed almost as though the Pole, now conquered, had surrendered all its defenses.

They made incredible time. April 9, they reached Bartlett's last camp—133 miles in less than three days. April 19, they sighted the distant mountains of Cape Columbia. April 22, they left the shifting sea ice, mounted once again the firm, steady glacial fringe that bordered the land itself.

Safe at last, the Eskimos went wild with delight. They yelled and danced until they fell in utter exhaustion. Sinking down on his sledge, Ootah could only say, "The devil is asleep or having trouble with his wife, or we should never have come back so easily."

Next morning they happily stumbled into Crane City—413 miles in just sixteen days. Here they collapsed in their igloos and slept the sleep of winners. They were utterly worn out; Peary had lost thirty pounds on the trip. But victory is a great medicine, and by April 25 they were revived and off on the final lap: two more long marches to Cape Sheridan and the *Roosevelt*.

On board, the Eskimos—always the first to see anything—began shouting and pointing at the distant figures advancing toward the ship. Bob Bartlett—usually the first to act—vaulted the rail and raced out on the ice. Extending his hand, he spoke with the breathless formality men sometimes use to hide their excitement: "I congratulate you, sir, on the discovery of the Pole!"

"How did you guess it?" laughed the commander.

But Bartlett changed the subject to the awful news that had haunted him for days: "Have you heard about poor Marvin?"

Of course Peary hadn't, and the story came out swiftly. Marvin had died, returning over the polar ice. No one knew exactly how it happened—only the story told by his shaken Eskimos, Kudlooktoo and "Harrigan." They reported that Marvin, traveling ahead of them both, had crashed through the thin ice of the "Big Lead." When they reached the spot, it was already too late to save him.

Peary was stunned. He admired Marvin greatly, and in addition this shook his professional pride. He considered himself the safest of Arctic explorers; until now he had lost only one man in eighteen years. It would have been small consolation had he known the story that came out later.

When Kudlooktoo was baptized in 1926 he confessed that Marvin had not drowned—he was shot. The Eskimo said he murdered the professor at the climax of a bitter dispute between Marvin and "Harrigan."

Whatever happened, everyone else was safe on the ship except MacMillan and Borup. They were on the Greenland coast laying down emergency supplies in case the polar party returned that way. Peary sent word to switch to tidal observations, then ordered them back at the first chance. With the great prize under his belt, he now wanted only to go home.

The *Roosevelt* finally cast off on July 18, began working her way south through the melting summer ice. The weather was still with them—Robeson Channel seemed a picnic compared to the trip up. As the ship steamed down the coast Borup and MacMillan led a giant walrus hunt. The Eskimos had missed their usual spring hunting to go with Peary, and the commander wasn't about to let them down now.

August 8, and the *Roosevelt* reached Nerke, first stop on the Greenland coast. Here they found three Eskimo families with some interesting news.

It seemed that while Peary was up at the Pole, Dr. Frederick A. Cook had reappeared. He was already gone again, so there was no way to know what he had been doing during his long disappearance. Peary tried asking the Eskimos, but they were very vague. Cook only told them he had been "a long way out on the sea ice . . . far north."

They learned much more when they reached Etah on August 17. Here they found their old "passenger" Harry Whitney, none the worse for his year of hunting in the wilderness. He was full of news about Cook.

The doctor had reappeared in April with two Eskimos and a sledge. They had come from Ellesmere Island across Smith Sound and were clearly exhausted from long, hard marching. Again, where had they been? Well, before heading on south to catch a whaling ship for Denmark, Cook told Whitney a momentous secret: He had reached the North Pole on April 21, 1908.

Peary was stunned. If true, it was a whole year before he got there—a sickening blow.

He quickly launched a little detective work. Borup examined Cook's sledge. It was hardly scratched. Certainly not battered the way it should be after a thousand miles across the polar ice. Henson and MacMillan interviewed Cook's two Eskimos—they laughed and said they were never far north, or even out of sight of land. They explained they had started north from Axel Heiberg Island and spent two nights about twenty miles out. Then they raised a flag over an igloo, headed south again, got lost, and wintered in Jones Sound. Come spring they returned via Ellesmere Island, as everyone knew.

Peary relaxed. He felt certain Cook had neither the experience nor the help to get all the way to the Pole; now his hunch seemed right. Still, he was bitter at the very thought of this man trying to rob him of the great prize. At first the ill-equipped Cook had seemed merely a fool; now that he was actually claiming victory, he seemed a cheat. Peary grew increasingly angry. When Whitney asked permission to carry back some of Cook's things on the *Roosevelt,* the commander coldly refused.

Continuing south, the ship reached Cape York on August 25. Here they left the last of their Eskimos—and found their first mail in over a

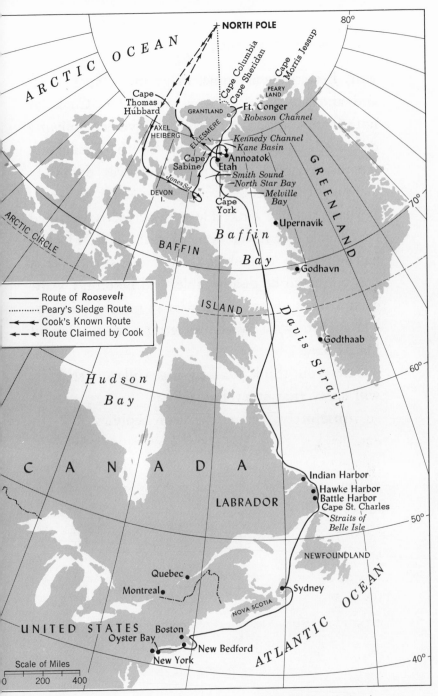

Graphic Presentation Services, Inc.

Peary's route and that claimed by Cook

year. Letters from home, magazines, papers . . . and another piece of news about Dr. Cook. A note from Captain Adams of the whaler *Morning* described meeting Cook in South Greenland. Adams reported that the doctor was definitely claiming the Pole.

Peary's heart sank. He was perfectly satisfied that Cook had never been near the Pole. He felt he could easily dispose of the doctor's story. Yet it was bound to be disagreeable, and he didn't want even a trace of unpleasantness to mar his victory. Thoughtfully he tossed the letter over to Donald MacMillan.

"Do you think," asked MacMillan, "that he will carry that story home?"

"Absolutely," came the grim reply.

IX   AN OLD FRIEND REAPPEARS

"Reached North Pole," Dr. Cook cabled the Brussels Observatory on September 1 from the little port of Lerwick in the Shetland Islands. He was now on his way back from Greenland, bound for Copenhagen on the blubber ship *Hans Egede*. This was the first port of call . . . the first chance to claim victory . . . the first word heard from the explorer since he disappeared north in the summer of 1907.

The world was electrified. Long before the *Hans Egede* reached Copenhagen, congratulations poured in from statesmen, scientists, universities, other explorers. The New York *Herald*, which turned out to have exclusive serial rights on the story, headlined the doctor's triumph and ran a brief summary he also cabled from Lerwick. It was pretty much the same story his Eskimos had told Peary. With one all-important exception— instead of camping in sight of land, Cook said the party had gone all the way north to the Pole.

Other newspapers, envying the *Herald* for its scoop, rushed their correspondents to Denmark. If they couldn't be the first to describe the doctor's triumph, they were certainly going to be on hand for the welcome. The whole world's attention focused on Copenhagen.

Little launches swarmed like waterbugs around the *Hans Egede* as she crept into Copenhagen harbor on the morning of September 4. Bands played, guns thundered, flags flew from every mast. Crowds lined the shore, wildly cheering the new hero. On the deck of the *Hans Egede* Dr. Cook stood happily taking the salute.

Crown Prince Christian of Denmark climbed aboard to give the royal greeting. United States Minister Egan presented Washington's compliments. Scores of eager reporters crowded around, copying everything the doctor had to say.

Ashore, he was swept up in a sea of cheering people. They escorted him to the Geographical Society, where he appeared on the balcony to take one more salute.

Nothing was too good for him. Tired of his rumpled clothes (they hadn't been pressed for two years), Dr. Cook had cabled from the ship asking for a new suit. When he reached his hotel rooms, he found racks of new suits waiting— every size and color, all his for the asking.

That evening he was received by the King of Denmark himself, and it seemed to be the final blessing on his triumph. The world took proper note. In America Governor Swanson of Virginia praised his dash and daring. Yale University hailed his victory. John Bradley, his original backer, declared that Cook's feat was "the most wonderful thing ever done by man."

Only here and there came a faint voice of doubt. Some Harvard professors, for instance, said they would like to see a little more proof. So did Peter Gibbs, a newspaper man from London.

But these skeptics were quickly squelched. Gibbs was even challenged to a duel.

Actually Dr. Cook needed no one to defend his honor. He seemed able to handle the doubters himself. "Let skeptics who disbelieve my story go to the North Pole," he declared. "There they will find a small brass tube which I have buried under the flag."

And whenever anyone asked about records, Dr. Cook had an answer here too. He had left his records with Harry Whitney in Greenland. And if anyone wondered how he could possibly have left such important evidence behind, the doctor merely assured everyone that he had copies and would produce them later.

But in the end his best support lay in his reception at Copenhagen. After all, these Scandinavians had the Arctic in their blood, and they should know. The Royal Danish Geographical Society gave him its gold medal for discovering the Pole. The Crown Prince presided over the ceremony. The explorer Knud Rasmussen endorsed him completely. Otto Sverdrup backed him to the hilt— and no one recalled that the great Norwegian was still smarting from that time in Kane Basin when Peary wouldn't have coffee with him.

The honors continued to pour in. On September 6 the occasion was a gala dinner at Copenhagen's famous Tivoli Casino. Dr. Cook was, of course, the guest of honor, nearly smothered in a garland of roses. But as he sat modestly blushing at the toasts and compliments, an electrifying rumor ran through the room—Peary was back, also claiming the Pole.

Dr. Cook heard, but no one could have guessed it. In his carefully prepared speech he made no mention of the rumor. He simply said once again how grateful he was to everybody, how much he owed to the Eskimos.

But he was ready afterward. As the correspondents rushed to the dais, the doctor faced them with a smile. . . .

What did he think of the news? "I am proud that a fellow American has reached the Pole. There is glory enough for us all."

Did he really believe Peary got there? "If Mr. Peary says he has discovered the Pole, I am sure he has."

Returning to New York on September 21, 1909, Dr. Frederick Cook was greeted by a cheering crowd. He later said, "I was conscious of confusion about me, of whistling and shrieking, of uncanny magnified voices thundering from scores of megaphones." At left is his wife, who hated publicity but soon found herself in the midst of one of the most violent controversies of the time.

Did he *really* think that way? "I am not a doubting Thomas . . . three cheers for him, the Stars and Stripes."

But wasn't Peary just a runner-up? "Two records are better than one . . . his observations and reports will confirm mine."

Back home the New York *Herald* nodded approvingly. By now the paper was committed to Cook, and his sportsmanship somehow backed up his case. "It is a foregone conclusion," the *Herald* added hopefully, "that Commander Peary will hail Dr. Cook's achievement in the same ungrudging spirit."

It wasn't going to be quite that easy. As the *Roosevelt* neared civilization again, Peary sternly told George Borup and Donald MacMillan, "Boys, say whatever you will, but please remember that there is to be no mention of Dr. Cook's name."

The commander was true to his own orders. When the ship reached Labrador on September 6 his first cables said absolutely nothing about Cook. But it was perfectly clear that Peary considered that he, and he alone, had discovered the North Pole.

"I have the Pole April 6," he cabled the *New*

York Times. "Stars and Stripes nailed to the Pole," ran his flash to the Associated Press. And then a special message to Mrs. Peary, "Have made good at last. I have the old Pole."

The news was a sensation—but not the way the commander intended. The world was not so much amazed by Peary's achievement, as by an incredible coincidence: after four hundred years of trying, two men had independently claimed the Pole within five days.

A flood of telegrams deluged the *Roosevelt.* What did Peary think about Cook? Was he satisfied with the doctor's claim? Did he agree that two records were better than one? Would he comment on the doctor's generosity in inviting Peary to share in the glory?

"Cook's story should not be taken too seriously," Peary cabled back on September 7. "The Eskimos who accompanied him say he went no distance north and not out of sight of land." That should stop the skeptics, he thought. But the questions continued.

"Don't let Cook's story worry you," the commander wired Mrs. Peary on September 8. "Have him nailed." That should fix it, he decided, but why couldn't they see there was nothing to Cook anyhow? His Eskimos' confession . . . his un-scratched sledge—it was all so obvious, but the queries still poured in.

"Do not trouble about Cook's story or attempt to explain any discrepancies in his statements," ran Peary's next blast. This one was a real block-buster, sent to the *New York Times* on September 9. "He has not been to the Pole on April 21,

At Captain Bartlett's urging, the *Roosevelt* was anchored at Battle Harbor, Labrador, where it underwent extensive clean-ing in preparation for Peary's return to New York. While they were there, representatives of the Associated Press, *Harper's Magazine,* seventeen reporters, five photographers, and a stenographer arrived to interview Peary. This picture shows Peary, wearing a broad-brimmed hat and standing slightly higher than the rest of the group, in an informal moment with the reporters, on September 16, 1909.

Culver Service

1908, or any other time. He has simply handed the public a gold brick."

Each message just fanned the flames. Reporters raced north to meet the *Roosevelt,* working her way down the Labrador coast. Peary finally decided to meet them all on September 16 in Mr. Croucher's twine loft at Battle Harbor.

The correspondents jammed in this little frame building. They crowded around the commander as he took his stand at one end of a musty hall. They fired salvo after salvo of questions and Peary answered them—quickly, briefly, but often bluntly too, for that was the way of the man.

When the meeting ended and the reporters rushed off, Peary felt he had settled everything. He had faced them, he had given them the facts. Perhaps he had seemed a little curt sometimes, but some of the questions were pretty stupid. And if he even seemed a little angry, he had a right to be. After all, Cook's story was so outrageous, so preposterous. Well, he had at last set them straight. Now they knew.

X "SOMEBODY OUGHT TO BE SPANKED"

The crew of the *Roosevelt* strained to hear the welcoming cheers. She was past the Statue of Liberty now, steaming up New York harbor on the morning of October 1. The big ovation should soon begin.

But all was silent. The port was busy honoring the three hundredth anniversary of Henry Hudson's voyage to America, and no one had time to notice the *Roosevelt*. Or almost nobody. As the ship steamed by a ferry, the crew did hear a few yells. But these were not cheers, they were jeers—

something about whether they met Cook coming back on their way up to the Pole.

The *Roosevelt* took her place in the great naval parade honoring Hudson. But it turned out to be no place of honor. Buried deep in the parade, the stubby black vessel seemed lost in the glittering line of cruisers and battleships.

Steaming up the river, Peary's men heard more noise now. Most of it unpleasant. Every passing excursion steamer seemed full of Cook supporters, calling out their taunts and jibes. Then to cap the humiliation, the *Roosevelt*—having weathered every Arctic peril—broke down in the middle of the Hudson and had to leave her place in line. More laughing insults.

The exasperated crew turned to shout back. But Peary sternly called a halt: "It does them more harm than it does us."

Brave words. Actually no one could have been hurt more than Peary by the taunts, and certainly none could have been more surprised. He was so sure he had stopped all this nonsense by his barrage of wires from Labrador. He felt so certain he had proved his own claims at the press conference in Mr. Croucher's twine loft. Yet here were the Cook people again, louder than ever.

It was perhaps inevitable. Peary simply wasn't made to be a good salesman. Tactless, he didn't like Dr. Cook and showed it. Blunt and uncompromising, he didn't think the doctor got anywhere near the Pole and flatly said so. Impatient, he didn't bother to spell out why. Proud of his own feat, he admitted it and ended up looking arrogant.

In contrast Dr. Cook was just what people wanted. He was so simple, friendly, and modest. And of course he was always so nice about Peary. "The Pole is big enough for two," he said generously.

Even after the fireworks began, Cook remained polite and unruffled. He stressed that he never complained about the commander seizing his supplies in Greenland. If the press happened to mention this, he hastily added, "Please don't say anything disagreeable about Peary."

No wonder the doctor had received such a roaring welcome when he reached New York on September 21. Cook fans jammed the excursion steamer *Grand Republic* and escorted him up the harbor. Over 100,000 people lined the waterfront. The Arctic Club gave him a huge banquet. Local officials handed him the keys to the city. Cheered on all sides, Dr. Cook went off to lecture across the country.

Meanwhile he picked up some excellent backing. America's two most venerable Arctic explorers, General Adolphus W. Greely and Admiral W. S. Schley, were loud in their praise. It was perhaps a coincidence that both had been grievously offended by Peary. The commander was openly scornful of Greely's work and had Schley's name erased from the maps. (True, Peary proved "Schleyland" was nonexistent, but he might have done it a little more tactfully.) In any case both of these distinguished warriors now wrote off Peary and jumped enthusiastically on the Cook bandwagon.

And it was really rolling by the time Peary reached New York. When a Pittsburgh newspaper polled its readers on who discovered the Pole, the vote came out Cook 73,238, Peary 2,814. A similar poll in Ohio gave Dr. Cook a 55-to-1 margin. At East Hampton, Long Island, a clergyman carefully put Cook's account in the cornerstone of his new church. He wanted it to be saved for the ages.

Peary watched all this in silent fury. He had been burned when he called the doctor's boast a "gold brick." The press had called him a poor sport then. Now he wasn't going to say anything at all. He resolved to wait until his records were examined and his own claim established.

But his friends were far from idle. They raked over Dr. Cook's discredited claim that he had been first to scale Mount McKinley. They rehashed old charges that the doctor had "stolen" a native language dictionary compiled by a missionary in Patagonia.

Cook's friends lashed back. Until now they had merely argued that Peary reached the Pole a poor second; soon they began hinting that he never got there at all. They pointed out that the only inspection of his instruments took place in a railroad baggage room. They showed he was sometimes fuzzy on his dates. Above all they insisted that he claimed to have sledged incredible distances. For Peary to have returned 133 miles on his first 3 marches from the Pole, he must have averaged 44 miles a day—yet the best previous explorers had made only 25 miles. It did no good for Peary to point out that he had revolutionized the whole technique of sledging . . . that under his system even inexperienced "tenderfeet" like Borup and MacMillan averaged 34 miles. The public knew only that competent authorities were dubious—the pros and cons were all too technical.

But there was nothing technical about the other charges raised against Peary. Everybody understood these—that he was a poor sport . . . that he wouldn't bring back Cook's belongings . . . that he charged $100 to rescue the doctor's scurvy-ridden assistant Rudolph Francke. And people lapped up stories that he was a tyrant to the Eskimos—a martinet who exploited them ruthlessly at the cost of a few pans and knives.

Only his own men (the stories ran) had been treated worse. Cook's supporters claimed that Peary didn't pay his men. They charged that he delayed writing Ross Marvin's mother. They said he shamefully mistreated the loyal Bob Bartlett in not taking him to the Pole . . . and it did no good for the captain to deny that his feelings were hurt.

Worst of all, Cook's friends pointed out, Peary had taken a Negro to the Pole. They claimed this was just a selfish device: he wanted the glory of being the first white man to get there. They ignored the very valid points that Matthew Henson was the most skillful sledge driver, the most experienced assistant, and easily the best at handling Eskimos.

The battle raged on. Soon no one was neutral. All the big newspapers and magazines chose sides. All the great experts were lined up, hurling broadsides at each other. Watching the uproar from the quiet sidelines of Newfoundland, Bob Bartlett's mother could only write her son, "I am beginning to think that somebody ought to be spanked. Send me a letter and let me know whether it's you or not."

Events gradually supplied the answer. First Harry Whitney returned, denying that Cook had left any records or polar observations with him. Then in October, Arctic expert George Kennan published two devastating articles attacking the doctor's sledge loads, times, and distances as completely impossible.

Next came an interesting discovery. Someone

The rival claims of Cook and Peary caused wild excitement everywhere. Some were completely baffled, as suggested by this cartoon from the Philadelphia *Record Herald*. The New York *World* remarked, "The question used to be 'What lies around the North Pole?' Now it is 'Who lies about it?'" Others felt they knew very well who really had discovered the Pole. In a poll conducted by the Pittsburgh *Press* in the fall of 1909, 73,238 readers favored Cook and 2,814 favored Peary.

noticed that Cook's "North Pole" picture showed the Eskimos wearing musk-oxen trousers. This was odd because the doctor himself said they killed none of these animals until the following winter at Jones Sound.

When Cook finally produced some computations on his trip, Admiral Colby M. Chester of the United States Navy offered an equally interesting set of figures. They showed that, to work out certain of his claimed observations, the doctor must have made the sun stand still for twelve days.

Later the *New York Times* came up with the biggest jolt of all. The paper uncovered two mathematicians who said they worked out Cook's polar observations in New York. The pro-Cook forces fought back—claimed the manufactured data was a Peary trap—but the country wasn't too sure.

By October 17 the harassed doctor canceled his lecture tour. Instead he concentrated on preparing his case. This he then sent to the University of Copenhagen. He had always said that the University was the final authority. Now he would await their decision.

It came on December 21. The University took

just two days' study to conclude that Dr. Cook's observations proved nothing. The official report was tactful, the committee members far less so. One called the data "shameless," another "most impudent."

So in the end Peary stood alone. Just as he had won the Pole, now he won the battle of claims and arguments.

But for a long while it was a hollow victory. This wasn't the way he had pictured it at all. He was much too romantic to want just a technical triumph; he wanted all the glory that went with it. He was much too proud to be content with vindication; he yearned for instant acceptance. None of this he would ever know. The sordid fight with Dr. Cook left a bitter taste that took years to rinse out.

Yet he did achieve his goal. He did prove that if a man tries long and hard enough, sometimes his dreams do come true. And without meaning to, he also confirmed a very old saying: Appearances can be deceiving. The stern, remote, difficult man is sometimes closer to being right than the one who is friendly and disarmingly convincing.

All this became ever more clear. In December,

1909, the National Geographic Society approved Peary's records and gave him its gold medal for discovering the Pole. One by one all the great scientific bodies followed suit—London on May 4, 1910 . . . Berlin on May 7 . . . Vienna on May 18.

That same day the world paused to take in a startling new phenomenon. The tail of Halley's Comet brushed the earth. Fortunetellers predicted the end of everything, Kansas farmers rushed to their cyclone cellars, and New Yorkers flocked to their skyscrapers to get a better view of doomsday.

Nothing happened, but wise men smiled to think of so much furor over something in the sky. Now that Peary had the Pole, they knew there was nothing exciting left to discover. None of them—not even the wisest—realized that his great feat was but one more step in the long staircase of discovery. None of them dreamed that Mr. Halley's bit of stardust could possibly be the herald of a whole new world to conquer.

BIBLIOGRAPHY

Books:

Bartlett, Robert A., THE LOG OF BOB BARTLETT. New York, G. P. Putnam's Sons, 1928.

Borup, George, A TENDERFOOT WITH PEARY. New York, Frederick A. Stokes Company, 1911.

Cook, Frederick A., MY ATTAINMENT OF THE POLE. New York, Mitchell Kennerly, 1913.

——— RETURN FROM THE POLE. Frederick J. Pohl, ed. New York, Pellegrini & Cudahy, 1951.

Freeman, Andrew A., THE CASE FOR DR. COOK. New York, Coward-McCann, Inc., 1961.

Freuchen, Peter, PETER FREUCHEN'S BOOK OF ARCTIC EXPLORATION. New York, Coward-McCann, Inc., 1962.

Gibbs, Philip, ADVENTURES IN JOURNALISM. New York, Harper & Brothers, Publishers, 1923.

Henson, Matthew A., A NEGRO EXPLORER AT THE NORTH POLE. New York, Frederick A. Stokes Company, 1912.

Hobbs, William Herbert, PEARY. New York, The Macmillan Company, 1936.

MacMillan, Donald B., HOW PEARY REACHED THE POLE. Boston, Houghton Mifflin Company, 1934.

Mirsky, Jeannette, TO THE NORTH. New York, The Viking Press, Inc., 1934.

Peary, Robert E., NEAREST THE POLE. New York, Doubleday, Page & Company, 1907.

——— THE NORTH POLE. New York, Frederick A. Stokes Company, 1910.

Stefansson, Vilhjalmur, THE FRIENDLY ARCTIC. New York, The Macmillan Company, 1921.

Weems, John Edward, RACE FOR THE POLE. New York, Henry Holt & Co., Inc., 1960.

Whitney, Harry Payne, HUNTING WITH THE ESKIMOS. New York, Century Publishing Company, 1911.

Periodicals:

Kennan, George, "Arctic Work and Arctic Food." *Outlook*, October 16, 1909.

——— "Commander Peary's Return." *Outlook*, October 2, 1909.

——— "Waiting for Peary." *Outlook*, September 25, 1909.

New York *Herald*, September–December, 1909.

New York Times, September–December, 1909.

INDEX

[Figures in italics indicate pages on which illustrations appear.]

(only copy)

919.8   Copy 2   5.00
Lor   12218

Lord, Walter
Peary to the pole

919.8   Copy 2   5.00
Lor   12218

Lord, Walter
Peary to the pole

DATE DUE	BORROWER'S NAME	ROOM NUMBER
MAR 07 91	Amy Radke	237
SEP 25	Danielle Archambault	123
OCT 15 91	Renew	

**Nauset Regional
Middle School Library**

RR 3 Route 28

Orleans, MA 02653

DEMCO